A Meath Anthology

COVER: detail from William Petty's *General Map of Ireland*, 1685

A Meath Anthology
is published in paperback
on 17 March 2010

by Meath County Council Library Service,
Railway Street, Navan, County Meath

www.meath.ie / library

ISBN 978 1 900923 24 8

DESIGNED BY HEXHIBIT

CONTENTS

Foreword

Tá traidisiún fada mórtais ag muintir An Mhí ina gceantar féin agus i stair, traidisiúin agus luachanna cultúrtha an cheantair sin. Gach uile bhliain, cuirtear lenár dtuiscint ar fhás agus ar fhorbairt ár gcontae, trí réimse leathan foilseachán – stair áitiúil, irisí, bliainirisí agus dialanna.

To the list of publications about Meath which yearly add to our understanding of the development of our county, it is a pleasure to add this anthology of poetry. It presents the engagement between poem makers and the landscape and people of the county which begins in the *Dindseanchas* and has been evolving since, but which has not previously been available in one volume.

We would like to thank the writers and publishers for their good will towards this project and for making their work available for publication. We would like to acknowledge the work of Meath County Council Library staff in preparing this book. It is hoped that *A Meath Anthology* will provide another means of seeing and engaging with the Royal County for all who live, work or visit here.

Cllr. William Carey
Cathaoirleach
Meath County Council
February 2010

Tom Dowling
County Manager
Meath County Council
February 2010

Introduction

Poetry and place: when literature and landscape rhyme

Meath means different things to different people. It is experienced differently by insiders and outsiders, tourists and locals, young and old, farmers and townspeople. Those who are born in the county are weighted with memories located in networks of family and friends. In-comers have pasts located elsewhere, but presents shaped by new encounters with Meath and its landscape. This book provides a medley of experiences of places in Meath. But its poetry is not exclusively about places – it is also about landscape sensations, sometimes profoundly personal musings, inspired by locality in Meath – a fusion of memory and place, in which the material, tangible landscape is the cue for recollection or reflection.

Landscapes can be written – in the bland factuality of journalism or the inventories of officialdom – or they can be represented as personal experience in which the gaze of the observer is foregrounded, often shaping our perception of the place observed. There is a balance between the nature of landscape and the nature of the writer's gaze, often to be discovered by readers in their engagement with the text.

Much of this book circles around landscapes and what might be called their 'placefulness', or their 'depth of place', springing from the way people encounter landscape in its present or past manifestations, and the way place provides a superstructure for personal reminiscence. Narrative constructions of landscapes by writers and poets have often a more real impact on readers than the material reality of earth, rocks or buildings in place.

Writers and artists are witnesses to our world, as well as being producers of it. In the same way that we acknowledge poets, for example, as having eloquence where most of us are inarticulate – expressing sublime human emotions like love or fear or longing – they also have an insight and deftness of expression in decoding the mystery of senses of place for us. Society honours its writers and poets who are often seen as interpreters of national culture, gifted with a talent to represent the times and spaces we live in. The power of the writer as witness is demonstrated by the manner in which Yeats, Heaney or Durcan are quoted approvingly in particular instances (at the inauguration of a President, for instance) to represent a state of mind about the Ireland or Irelands we live in. In the same way in the United States, the poets Robert Frost and Elizabeth Alexander were invited to recite, the one at the Kennedy, the other at the Obama inaugurations.

Creative artists like poets, therefore, are valuable interpreters of our worlds in the past and the present whose work adds the flesh of meaning to what are often the bald facts of place. Our past and present views of Irish or regional or local landscapes have been shaped to a great extent by renditions of literature and art. The Romantic or Impressionist movements in art formed a cultural, social, even an economic frame of reference for popular perspectives on reality. The public was conditioned into looking for certain kinds of landscape reality or experience – wild exotic landscapes in the early nineteenth century or the dripping river pastures with ruins in Constable's Suffolk. In a similar way, our expectations about the West of Ireland, or the rural idyll more generally, have been influenced in one way or another by art and writing in the past century.

We can also talk about the way signatures of local landscape are inscribed in the work of writers/artists who have deep associations with a region or landscape. This is well represented in Patrick Kavanagh's poetry on Iniskeen and south Monaghan which contains a strong topographical awareness of the dripping drumlin landscapes of hills and streams, fields and farms: 'To know fully even one field or lane is a lifetime's experience. In the poetic world it is depth that counts and not width. A gap in a hedge, a smooth rock surfacing a narrow lane, a view of a woody meadow, the stream at the juncture of four small fields – these are as much as man can fully experience.'[1]

Kavanagh was an acute observer and interpreter of landscape in its day-to-day ordinariness and mundanity:

'*The wind leans from Brady's, and the coltsfoot leaves are holed
    with rust,
Rain fills the cart-tracks and the sole-plate grooves;
A yellow sun reflects in Donaghmoyne
The poignant light in puddles shaped by hooves.*'[2]

Kavanagh's 'Bluebells for Love', however, (reprinted in this book) is a much more transient acquaintance (with Dunsany) that is loaded with emotional depth that probably cannot be plumbed by its readers today. So landscape and literature rhyme at different levels for different writers in a variety of circumstances – and they rhyme differently too for the readers who come to them.

It is also notable that the art of writing constructs places of the imagination. While 'literary landscapes' obviously spring from an author's lived experience, they also represent imaginatively constructed locations that exist only in the mind of the writer. Even the most prosaic ballad of

---

[1] *Patrick Kavanagh: Man and Poet*, (ed.) Peter Kavanagh: National Poetry Foundation, University of Maine at Orono, 1986, p. 15.

[2] Patrick Kavanagh, *The Great Hunger*, MacGibbon & Kee, 1964, p. 36.

hunting or racing in this book contains flights of fantasy and topographic hyperbole, with local geographies tweaked to fit the needs of narrative or the conventions of rhyme. Wordsworth's rugged landscapes were amalgams of many locations in the English Lake District. Goldsmith's Deserted Village has been characterised as a fictive place but poets have the privilege of (re)constructing/(re)producing places of the imagination, undoubtedly in Goldsmith's case strongly influenced by memories of his Westmeath childhood.

It has been said that fictive reality in a poem or novel may contain more truth than the territorial or everyday reality of a landscape. Good writing on landscape, locality or place uses the power of language to summon up images of the texture of place, evoking an atmosphere and sense of place, reflected perhaps in the sounds or light of the landscape, in its essential wetness, coldness or dampness, darkness or sunlight. Layers of emotion and memory too add depth to the palimpsest of landscape that escapes ordinary pedestrian encounters.

At the same time, much earlier writing on landscape was, comparatively speaking, topographically accurate in its attempt to articulate the spirit and texture of place in an age before the revolution in visual imagery which came with photography, cinema and television. Eighteenth and nineteenth-century poetry for instance is often authentically descriptive, as in Goldsmith's commentary on landscape changes in his time – such as the clearance of small farms to make way for gentry parklands. We still await a literary response to the environmental or cultural impact of the M3 in its progress through the heartland of Meath.

This book is peppered with the poetry of placenames of Meath, important markers of locality and identity and indicators of depth of place for local writers –what Seamus Heaney has characterised as 'posts to fence out a personal landscape.'[3] : Boyne, Tara, Skene, Blackwater, Nanny, Allenstown, Archerstown, Bellewstown, Bettystown, Ballivor, Clonmellon, Curraha, Dunshaughlin, Dunsany, Moynalty, Drumree, Kilbrew, Loughcrew, Clonee, Culmullen, Killallon, Rathmanoe, Corbalton, Muchwood, Dunboyne, Balrath, Batterstown, Summerville, Rossnaree, Newgrange, Clavanstown, Balreask, Lagore, Rathkenny, Moydorragh, Oristown, Caultown, Tullyard, Kilskeer, Rathmore, Kilmainham, Longwood, Laracor, Headfort, Kingsfort, Cruisetown, Balnavoran.

So what does Meath mean and how does it appear in the following writings? It means rich grazing lands, low hills with the mighty Boyne 'curling imperturbably' (in the words of Seamus Heaney) through pastures knee-deep in grass, enclosed in house-high hedges, fenced with towering beech, ash and chestnut. In spite of the iconic landscapes of Tara and Newgrange, much of Meath has hidden, secret places, occasions for quiet reverie for Paul Durcan –

> '...along empty roads
> in the haze of a May morning.
> Crossroads after empty crossroads.'

This is pre-eminently cattle country. F.R. Higgins's 'herds hid in their own breathing', where Padraic Colum's drover recalls

> '... the smell of the beasts,
>   the wet wind in the morn,
> and the proud and hard earth
>   never broken for corn.'

---

3   Seamus Heaney, 'Sense of Place' in *Preoccupations*, Faber, 1984, p. 141.

Meath is, of course, a myth-marked landscape embedded in history and legend: Tara, Slane, Skryne, Sliabh na gCaillighe, Brú na Bóinne – Lynda Moran's 'stones celebrating some mystery', or Heaney's dawn light 'stealing/ through the cold universe to county Meath', or where in Peter Fallon's words

> 'Past and present join
> in the winter solstice.
> The days will stretch and we survive ...'

Even though the Anglo-Normans had colonised and transformed the territory of Meath, tradition persisted into the early modern period invoking sagas of earlier/ancient worlds of Aengus and Cormac and the symbolic power of their landscape inscriptions. For Kinsella, through the mists of Tara

> 'A horse appeared at the rampart like a ghost,
> and tossed his neck at ease, with a hint of harness'.

Meath is also about castles, mottes, and walled towns of Trim and Kells, landscapes pockmarked with ruins although the shapes and patterns and ancient street lines endure from the past. The ruins are the legacies of a fractured history commemorated in Longley's 'broken stones' and the haunted ruins of Kinsella's *King John's Castle*:

> 'Life, a vestigial chill, sighs along the tunnels
> through the stone face. The great collapsed rooms, the mind
> of the huge head, are dead. Views open inward
> on empty silence; a chapel-shelf, moss-grown, unreachable.'

★

Meath is a microcosm of the long-settled, man-handled, intimately-known Irish landscape, a legacy of generations of investment in construction and remembering. Sean O Faoláin acknowledged the depth of place of his Irish homeland in 1929 as he pondered the sublime landscapes of the Rio Grande and Rockies: "...there was not a soul in sight; ...we were oppressed by the silence... There wasn't even the least cry of a bird. It was an immeasurable night. And it wasn't in the least bit impressive – because if these mountains had associations we did not know them; if history – that is, if some purposeful life, other than of missionaries or explorers, ever trod this vastness – it had left no vibrations... we belonged to an old, small, intimate and much trodden country, where every field, every path, every ruin had its memories, where every last corner had its story. We decided that we could only live in Europe and in Ireland."[4]

Meath is such a well-trodden, richly endowed human landscape.

Patrick Duffy,
Dept. of Geography, NUI Maynooth, February 2010

---

[4] Sean O'Faoláin, *Vive Moi! An Autobiography,* Hart-Davis, 1965, p. 241.

A Note on the Text

The hunt for the poems collected here was prompted by
an absence and a curiosity. The absence was the one book
where writing about the people and landscape of Meath in
the form of poetry had been gathered. The curiosity was
about the myriad of places that make up Meath, and about
the poets who had yielded to the temptation to pull into the
hard shoulder, stray from the beaten path and head off into
the landscape.

That curiosity extended to whether those poets had, in their
peregrinations, been as fortunate to find in the great fortress
of Meath the 'valour, hospitality, and truth; / bravery, purity,
and mirth' that Alfred, the Northumbrian monarch-in-exile,
found here in the 7th century.

Over time the search yielded poems and, when the
individual sheets had thickened to a sheaf, the next natural
step appeared to be to consider them in relation to each
other and to speculate on whether the disparate poems
might be brought together to constitute a volume in its own
right.

The main criterion in placing the poems to establish
a semblance of order was to avoid any grouping by
chronology or geography or register, to encourage the living
and the dead to break bread together, and to allow high art
to rub shoulders with folk song and popular street ballad.

This gathering opens by placing the oldest poem we could
find – from the 12th century Book of Leinster – with the
newest, as yet uncollected and transmitted by electronic
mail in the 21st century. Many of the poems are juxtaposed
for their contrasting styles, jumping-off points and subject
matter. Others poems are placed together for the way they
approach similar subject matter in completely different ways

– Michael Longley and Máirtín Ó Direáin regarding Saint Oliver Plunkett's head in Drogheda, springs to mind.

Where translations from the original Irish existed we were happy to have them appear alongside the original. Where no translation existed – or at least none that we knew of that did the original justice, as in the case of Séamus Dall Mac Cuarta's *Iomáin na Bóinne* – the original stands unaccompanied.

I am happy to acknowledge a debt of gratitude to Frances Tallon in the preparation of this text. Her clear-eyed reading and attention to detail are everywhere to be seen.

Finally, it seemed only right to grant the last word to Meath's foremost contemporary exponent of the singing line and to have the book conclude with the 'to live; to thrive' of his *A Winter Solstice*. What more could anybody hope for?

Tom French, Navan, February 2010

MIDE

Mide magen na marc mer,
slige forsmbíd Art Oen-fer,
lerg lán lainne Lugdech luid,
clár clainne Chuind is Chobthaig.

Cid diatá Mid ar in maig,
fine síl Chuind chét-chathaig?
cia gass glúair garg, glan in mod,
cia harg ó fúair ainmnigod?

Mide mac bruthmar Bratha
meic dirmannaig Deatha,
co roatái tenid ndiamair
ós chlaind Nemid nert-giallaig.

Secht mbliadna lána ar lassad
don tenid, ba trén-fassad,
corscáil gairge in tened trell
tar cethri hairde hÉrend.

Conid ón tenid-sin tra,
(ní hanfót ní himmarba)
condlig a sír-chennach ind
cach prím-thellach in Érind.

Condlig a chomarba cain
maige Midi medar-glain
miach móeth-bleithe la muic find
cacha hóen-cleithe in Érind.

Co roráidset, nír sním súail,
drúide hÉrend i n-óen-úair,
"Is mí-dé tucad dún tair,
dorat mí-gné d'ar menmain."

3

Corthinól Mide cen meth
drúide hErend i n-óen-tech:
co tall a tengtha, túar ngarg,
a cendaib na ndrúad ndron-ard.

Co rosadnaicc fo thalmain
Uisnig Midi mór-adbail,
co ndessid ar a tengthaib
in prím-súi in prím-senchaid.

Gáine ingen Gumóir glain,
muime Midi mid-charthaig,
ba ferr cach mnái, ciarbo thúi,
ba sái ba fáith ba prím-drúi.

Co n-erbairt Gáine co n-úaill
re Mide cosin mór-búaid:
"Is ós neoch rosníad ar tech
conid deseo bías Uisnech."

Uisnech ocus Mide múad
asngabar hÉriu arm-rúad,
feib adfét in súidi snas,
is desin a dind-senchas.

Dín, a Dé, Aéd úa Carthaig
ar iffern co méit anfaid:
Dia d' iráil a grésa glé
for ríg mid-charthach Mide.

Aed úa Carthaig

MIDE

Mide, place of the eager steeds,
the road whereon Art the Solitary used to be,
the lowland full of the splendour of Lugaid …
the level ground of the clan of Conn and Cobthach.

Whence is the name of Meath given to the plain?
To the heritage of the seed of Conn the Hundred Fighter?
What pure, bold scion, (bright the hero),
What warrior was it whence it got its naming?

Mide it was, the ardent son of Brath,
the host-leading son of Deaith;
for he kindled a mystic fire
above the race of Nemed, seizer of hostages.

Seven years good ablaze
was the fire, it was a sure truce:
So that he shed the fierceness of the fire for a time
over the four quarters of Erin.

So that it is from this fire in truth
(it is not a rash saying, it is not a falsehood)
that their head-man has a right for ever
over every chief hearth of Erin.

So the right belongs to the gentle heir
of the plain of Mide mirthful and bright;
even a measure of fine meal with a white pig
for every rooftree in Erin.

And they said, (no small grief it was),
The druids of Erin all together,
"It is an ill smoke was brought to us eastward:
It has brought an ill mood to our mind."

Then Mide, the untiring, assembled
the druids of Erin into one house,
and cut their tongues (a harsh presage)
out of the heads of the strong and noble druids.

And he buried them under the earth
of Uisneach in mighty Mide,
and sat him down over their tongues,
he, the chief seer and chief poet.

Gaine, daughter of pure Gumor,
nurse of mead-loving Mide,
surpassed all women though she was silent;
she was learned and a seer and a chief druid.

And Gaine said with lamentation,
before Mide of the great victory,
"It is 'over somewhat' our house was built,
And hence shall Uisneach be named."

Uisneach and mighty Mide
from which Erin of the red weapons is held,
according as the learned relate the cutting,
hence is derived its story.

Guard, O God, Aed úa Carthaig
from hell with all its storms,
God enjoining his clear protection
on the mead-loving king of Meath.

      Aed úa Carthaig

Capital

for Catherine and Patrick

At the river field's five-barred gate
a rust brown spate
of Angus and Hereford
mullocked and shouldered
through our unplanned, half-lit meanders
across Fyanstown's seemingly trackless acres,
showing us what is always to hand,
the lay of the land,
its bullshit
and its cowshit
and its cow roads that saunter,
with the flow, natural
as Tara's ancient capital
and the flat, invisible Blackwater.

John McAuliffe

TARA

The mist hung on the slope, growing whiter
on the thin grass and dung by the mounds;
it hesitated at the dyke, among briars.

Our children picked up the wrapped flasks, capes and baskets
and we trailed downward among whins and thrones
in a muffled dream, guided by slender axe-shapes.

Our steps scattered on the soft turf, leaving
no trace, the children's voices like light.
Low in the sky behind us, a vast silver shield

seethed and consumed itself in the thick ether.
A horse appeared at the rampart like a ghost,
and tossed his neck at ease, with a hint of harness.

Thomas Kinsella
from *Nightwalker and other poems,* The Dolmen Press, 1968

from KING ALFRED'S POEM

I found in the fair-surfaced Leinster,
from Dublin to Sliabh Mairge,
long-living men, health, prosperity,
bravery, hardihood, and traffic.

I found from Ara to Gle,
in the rich country of Ossory,
sweet fruit, strict jurisdiction,
men of truth, chess-playing.

I found in the great fortress of Meath
valour, hospitality, and truth;
bravery, purity, and mirth,
the protection of all Ireland.

I found the aged of strict morals,
the historians recording truth.
Each good, each benefit that I have sung,
in Ireland I have seen.

*from a 9th century poem by the Northumbrian King Alfred
during his Irish exile in about 685 AD*

THE EIGHTH WONDER OF IRELAND

I

Giraldus Cambrensis recounted the seven wonders
of Ireland. Hot hedge, impenetrable pale
on fire, up, down, around, between and under,
protecting the holy virgins from our male
intrusion at Kildare. Bell, with a stoop,
hobbling in round of mercy from the belfry
at Fore. Delight of priest and deacon, stoop
that brims with wine for daily Mass. Steep, self-
descending, ten-mile-sounding, ship-devouring,
green, glassy, walling Whirlpool. Bull-man
mounting in turn twelve crummies, glowering
in field. Cross in the parish of Ratoath
that spoke against false witness on oath.
Tincture of island clay that cures the bite
of reptile, adder, lessens ayen-bite.

II

To the seven wonders of Ireland, add an eighth.
Thrones and Dominions have changed our copybooks.
Crooked is straight, upside is down, pothooks
are hangers, good is bad now, pity, cruel,
free medicine, school-milk, contrary to Faith;
the old, the sick, cannot have soup or fuel,
parents, who anguish vainly to support
their infants, are robbed of them unhomed in Court,
pelfing is grace, substance of self, a wraith.

Austin Clarke
from *Flight to Africa and Other Poems*,
The Dolmen Press, 1963

CAROLAN'S APOLOGY TO CIAN ÓG O'HARA (SEÁN HARLÓ)

18th century

As I was of a Tuesday on the street at Droichead Mór
who should bump into me but John Harlow, and he stewed,
with a bottle of good whiskey that he shoved into my fist –
and God help us, but I said that he was better than O'Hara!

Another day and I was in the tavern drinking ale.
A frightful crock came on me and a rambling in my speech.
Why wouldn't some kind neighbour squeeze a padlock
    round my throat
when I ever put John Harlow on a level with O'Hara?

You make me screech with horror, John, you bloody
    monstrous whale!
You ugly lump of lowness, with the creaking in your pipe!
The time you're scoffing flummery and guzzling penny beer,
there'll be Spanish wine and claret on the table for O'Hara!

John V. Kelleher
from *Too Small for Stove Wood, Too Big for Kindling*,
The Dolmen Press, 1979

THE SHAMROCK HOTEL

Come you true sons of Erin that want a repose,
just step into Longwood and you'll get a fine dose.
Call into Montgomery's, they will treat you right well
in that grand lodging house called *The Shamrock Hotel*.

It's for ages this mansion has held up its name
for indulging the blind and for helping the lame.
While Mary gets the coppers and Mick rings the bell
and them all keeping time in *The Shamrock Hotel*.

From all parts of Ireland they come here to sleep –
the cooper, the hooper, the tinker, the sweep.
There's Kennedy and Irwin, Tint Pole and Mad Nell,
and they all flock like crows to *The Shamrock Hotel*.

On the last ship that landed there sailed home a yank,
a well-to-do tradesman with money in bank.
At the last fair of Longwood he cut a great swell
with batter-faced Mag from *The Shamrock Hotel*.

There is Mrs. Gough. She got a terrible fright
when she met a big tramp in the dead of the night.
To make matters worse he was stripped to his pelt
and he chasing a bug that ran off with his belt.

When the soldiers and peelers came to the scene
they ordered the beds to be thrown on the green.
Mag fell a fainting and Mick roared like hell –
"We've lost all we made in The Shamrock Hotel."

This beautiful mansion is going to be sold
to the Princess of Wales for ten guineas in gold.
The haggard, the stables and the boglands as well,
they are all going in with *The Shamrock Hotel*.

Patrick Cullen, Clondalee, Hill of Down

SKREEN CROSS ROADS

Five roads meet on the hill of Skreen,
five fair ways to wander down.
One road sings of the valleys green,
two of the sea, and one of the town.
And one little road has never a song
Tho' the world be fair and the day be long.

This is the song the south road sings:
'I go where Love and Peace abide.
I pass the world's seven wondrous things
and cities fallen in their pride.
Sunny are the miles thro' which I stray
from the Southern Cross to the Milky Way.'

But for all its song is so sweet to hear
it has no melody for my ear.

This is the song the sea road sings:
'When the moon is full the tide is high;
and the little ships in the harbours swing
when the sea-birds tell that a storm is nigh,
and "Heave" the sailor calls, and "Ho!"
It is far to my love when the strong winds blow.'

Oh the lure of the roads that sing of the sea
make my heart beat fast till it breaks in me.

This is the song of the road to the town:
'Row by row stand the silent lights,
and the music of bells goes up and down
the slopes of the wind, and high delights
lure in the folk from the valley farms.
It pulls down the hills with its great, grey arms.'

It sings its song so low and sweet
that once or twice it has lured my feet.

But the dumb little road that winds to the north
is the dearest road in the world to me.
I would give my soul – for what it is worth –
to be there in its silent company,
telling it over my hopes and fears,
with only its silence consoling my ears.

Francis Ledwidge
in hospital in Egypt, 3 April, 1916

AN LON DUBH BÁITE

A iníon álainn Choinn Uí Néill
   is fada do shuan tar éis d'áir;
Is nach gcluin uaisle do chine féin
   tú ag caoineadh do spré tar éis a bháis.

Ceiliúr an éin lúfair luaith,
   theastaigh uait, a fhaoileann bhán;
cha bhíonn tubaiste ach mar mbíonn spré,
   is déansa foighid ó ghreadadh lámh.

Ó ghreadadh lámh is ó shileadh rosc,
   glacsa tost, a fhaoileann úr;
A iníon álainn Choinn Uí Néill,
   fá bhás an éin ná fliuch do shúil.

A fhaoileann a d'fhás ó ardrí Uladh na rí,
   fuirigh mar tá, is fearr é nó imeacht le baois;
fá d'éan beag a b'áille gáire ar imeall na gcraobh,
   chan ceist a bhás go brách is é nite le haol.

Séamus Dall Mac Cuarta (c. 1650–1732/3)

Lovely daughter of Conn Ó Néill,
   sleep long after your great loss.
Don't let your noble kinsmen hear you
   weeping after your treasure's death.

The song of that swift, nimble bird
   is gone for good, my beauty pale.
But where's the treasure brings no trouble?
   Hold a while, don't beat your hands.

Not beaten hands and streaming eyes
   but silence, my noble beauty.
Lovely daughter of Conn Ó Néill,
   the bird is dead, don't wet your eyes.

O beauty, grown from kings of royal Ulster,
   be steady now; it is better than raving wild.
Your small bird laughing loveliest on the bough-tips,
   fret no more for his death: he is washed in lime.

(translated by Thomas Kinsella)

PAUD O'DONOHOE

When the Yeos were in Dunshaughlin and the Hessians in
	Drumree,
and spread through fair Moynalty's plain were the Fencibles
	of Reagh,
when Roden's godless troopers reigned from Skryne to
	Mullacroo
and hammered were the pike heads first by Paud
		O'Donohoe.

Young Paud he was as brave a boy as ever hammer swung,
and the finest hurler that you'd find in the lads of Meath
	among.
And when the wrestling match was o'er no man could
	boast he threw
the black-haired smith of Curraha, young Paud O'Donohoe.

But '98's dark season came and Irish hearts were sore,
the pitchcap and the triangle the patient fold outwore,
Young Paud, he thought of Ireland and said *"There's work to do."*
"We'll forge some steel for freedom", said Paud O'Donohoe.

And at Curraha each night you'd hear his anvil ring
while scouting on the roadside were Hugh and Phelim King,
with Duffy's Matt and Mickey's Pat and Hughie Gilsenan too,
while in the forge for Ireland worked young Paud O'Donohoe.

But a traitor crept amongst them and the secret soon was sold
to the captain of the Yeomen for his ready Saxon gold,
and a troop rushed out one evening from the woods of
	lone Kilbrew
and soon a rebel prisoner bound was Paud O'Donohoe.

"Down on your knees, you rebel dog", the Yeoman captain roared,
and high above his silvered crest he waved his gleaming sword.
"Down on your knees to meet your doom; such is the rebel's due."

But straight as pikestaff 'fore him stood young Paud
    O'Donohoe.

And there upon the roadside where in childhood he had played
before the cruel yeoman he stood quite undismayed.
"I kneel but to my God above, I ne'er shall bow to you.
You can shoot me as I'm standing", said Paud O'Donohoe.

The captain gazed in wonder, then lowered his keen-edged blade.
"A rebel bold is this", he said. *"He's fitting to degrade."*
"Here, men! Unbind him. My charger needs a shoe.
The king shall have a workman in Paud O'Donohoe."

Now to the forge young Paud has gone, Yeomen guard the
    door,
and soon the angry bellows is heard to snort and roar.
The captain stands with rein in hands while Paud he fits the
    shoe,
and when it's on 'tis short the shrift he'll give O'Donohoe.

The last strong nail is firmly clinched, the captain's horse is
    shod.
"Now rebel bold, thine hour has come. Prepare to meet thy God."
But why holds he the horse's hoof? There's no more work
    to do.
Why clenches he the hammer so? Young Paud O'Donohoe.

A leap! A roar! A smothered groan. The captain drops the rein
and sinks to earth with hammer head sunk deeply in his brain,
and lightly in the saddle, fast running towards Kilbrew
upon the captain's charger sits bold Paud O'Donohoe.

A volley from the muskets, a rush of horses' feet,
he's gone and none can capture the captain's charger fleet.
And in the night winds backward come a mocking loud halloo,
which tells the Yeomen they have lost young Paud O'Donohoe.

And still in Meath's fair county there are brave lads, not a few,
who would follow in the footsteps of Paud O'Donohoe.

Patrick Archer
The Nation newspaper, 1843

KING JOHN'S CASTLE

Not an epic, being not loosely architectured,
    but with epic force, setting the head spinning
with the taut flight earthward of its bulk, King John's
    Castle rams fast down the county of Meath.
This in its heavy ruin. New, a brute bright plateau,
    it held speechless under its cold a whole province of Meath.

Now the man-rot of passages and broken window-casements,
    vertical drops chuting through three storeys of masonry,
draughty spiral stairways loosening in the depths,
    are a labyrinth in the medieval dark. Intriguers
who prowled here once into the waiting arms
    of their own monster, revisit the blowing dust.

Life, a vestigial chill, sighs along the tunnels
    through the stone face. The great collapsed rooms, the mind
of the huge head, are dead. Views open inward
    on empty silence; a chapel-shelf, moss-grown, unreachable.
King John directs at the river a grey stare, who once
    viewed the land in a spirit of moderation and massacre.

Contemplatives, tiny as mice moving over the green
    mounds below, might take pleasure in the well
of quiet there, the dark foundations near at hand.
    Up here where the wind sweeps bleakly, as though in
        remembrance
against our own tombstones, the brave and great might gather.
    For the rest, this is not their fortress.

    Thomas Kinsella
    from *Another September*, The Dolmen Press, 1958

All travellers at first incline
Where'er they see the fairest sign,
And if they find the chambers neat,
And like the liquor and the meat,
Will call again, and recommend
The Angel Inn to every friend.
And though the painting grows decay'd,
The house will never lose its trade:
Nay, though the treach'rous tapster, Thomas,
Hangs a new Angel two doors from us,
As fine as daubers' hands can make it,
In hopes that strangers may mistake it,
We think it both a shame and sin
To quit the true old Angel Inn.
　　Now this is Stella's case in fact,
An angel's face a little crack'd.
(Could poets or could painters fix
How angels look at thirty-six:)
This drew us in at first to find
In such a form an angel's mind;
And every virtue now supplies
The fainting rays of Stella's eyes.
See, at her levee crowding swains,
Whom Stella freely entertains
With breeding, humour, wit, and sense,
And puts them to so small expense;
Their minds so plentifully fills,
And makes such reasonable bills,
So little gets for what she gives,
We really wonder how she lives!
And had her stock been less, no doubt
She must have long ago run out.
　　Then, who can think we'll quit the place,
When Doll hangs out a newer face?
Nail'd to her window full in sight

All Christian people to invite,
Or stop a light at Chloe's head,
With scraps and leavings to be fed?
    Then, Chloe, still go on to prate
Of thirty-six and thirty-eight;
Pursue your trade of scandal-picking,
Your hints that Stella is no chicken;
Your innuendoes, when you tell us,
That Stella loves to talk with fellows:
But let me warn you to believe
A truth, for which your soul should grieve;
That should you live to see the day,
When Stella's locks must all be gray,
When age must print a furrow'd trace
On every feature of her face;
Though you, and all your senseless tribe,
Could Art, or Time, or Nature bribe,
To make you look like Beauty's Queen,
And hold for ever at fifteen;
No bloom of youth can ever blind
The cracks and wrinkles of your mind:
All men of sense will pass your door,
And crowd to Stella's at four-score.

    Jonathan Swift

I REMEMBER SIR ALFRED

The gardens of Buckingham Palace
were strewn once with Irish loam
so those English moles that knew their place
would have no sense of home.

Watching Irish navvies drinking pints
this evening in Camden Town
I remember Sir Alfred McAlpine –
the shortest distance between two points
is a straight line.

The spirit of Sir Alfred McAlpine
paces the meadow, and fixes his theodolite
on something beyond the horizon,
love, or fidelity.

Charles Stewart Parnell, the I.R.A.,
redheaded women, the way back to the digs,
the Irish squire
who trained his spy-glass
on a distant spire
and imagined himself to be attending Mass.

Now Sir Alfred has dislodged a hare
that goes by leaps and bounds
across the grazing,
here and there,
this way and that, by singleminded swervings.

Paul Muldoon
from *Why Brownlee Left*, Faber & Faber, 1980

SHANLOTHE

You could set your watch
by the fields around Shanlothe
on warm summer evenings when
creosote dribbles down the gate posts

and the rocks in the river bed
are painted dry by July.
Half past eight and the hawk hangs no hands
above the acropolis of Neville's old house.

He's spoiled for choice and opts for
a colossus of copper beech. Ten minutes later
it will be nearing nine when the big shorthorns
begin to elbow their way

through the sheep on Canty's Hill.
By ten all will have disappeared under
an avalanche of night
and only the moon will strike the hour
over the pyramids of Egypt.

Tommy Murray
from *Counting Stained Glass Windows*, Lapwing, 2009

March 1, 1847. By the First Post.

The daffodils are out & how
you would love the harebells by
the Blackwater now.
But Etty, you are wise to stay away.
London may be dull in this season.
Meath is no better I assure you.
Your copper silk is sewn
& will be sent & I envy you.
No one talks of anything but famine.
I go nowhere –
not from door to carriage – but a cloth
sprinkled with bay rum & rose attar
is pressed against my mouth.
Our picnics by the river –
remember that one with Major Harris? –
our outings to the opera
& our teas
are over now for the time being.
Shall I tell you what I saw on Friday,
driving with Mama? A woman lying
across the Kells Road with her baby –
in full view. We had to go
out of our way
to get home & we were late
& poor Mama was not herself all day.

Eavan Boland
from *In a Time of Violence*, Carcanet Press, 1994

Balnavoran

"The memory of the brightest joys,
In childhood's happy morn that found us,
Is dearer than the richest toys
The present vainly sheds around us."

— Griffin

I

Last eve I strayed beyond the lake,
the west wore tints bright golden,
but, ah! my soul was sadly filled
    with recollections olden;
the damson groves were snowy white,
    and yet I fain would mourn
the sight I saw 'mid Nature's bloom –
    'twas ruined Balnavoran.

II

Some time ago it was a place
    that cheered my soul to enter –
the cosy cots that circled round,
    the chapel in the centre,
where Father Reilly preached and prayed,
    and soothed the heart forlorn.
Now weeds and crumbling walls alone
    remain in Balnavoran!

III

Ah me! How changed – that straw-clad dome
    was then our rustic college,
where I from poor Ned Smyth received
    my scanty store of knowledge.

But he – God rest his guiltless soul –
    has found the last sad bourne.
He sleeps beyond in Enniskeen,
    far, far from Balnavoran.

IV

A mother's love, a father's smile -
    the bright stars of our childhood!
Beneath them spring the sweetest flowers
    that scent life's tangled wild wood;
these are the boons too early lost,
    from me too early torn.
They then illumed my humble home
    near darling Balnavoran.

V

Here stood the village grocer's store
    with signboard blue and yellow
that lured in youth my longing gaze
    with sugar brown and mellow.
'Tis now a fallen edifice,
    of all its glories shorn.
There's naught to sell and few to buy
    in poor old Balnavoran.

VI

John Caffrey then was well to do
    in cattle and in tillage,
and all who knew him owned him lord
    and ruler of the village;
his boots shone glossy black, his spurs
    a prince might well have worn.

He's now a breadless pauper lodged
near roofless Balnavoran.

VII

Owen Fagan, too, was deemed a man
a lady might admire,
and many a jig I've seen him dance,
well played by Mick Maguire.
His dress, once neat as frieze could be,
is scanty, old and torn.
A crutch sustains his thin, spare limbs
today in Balnavoran.

VIII

And where's the colleen bawn I loved
with boyhood's blissful ardour?
I, lonely, seek the silent glen
where first my heart adored her.
The thorn hedge stands, the brook runs by,
the grass-green robes are worn
by flowery dells, but she's not there
to gladden Balnavoran.

IX

Departed loved ones, some have fled,
whose golden worth snatched from us,
have found beyond the western wave
a land of faithless promise;
while hate and scorn are *there* endured
which *here* too long were borne,
a holy grave were better far
near ruined Balnavoran!

x

And I, even I, who sadly sing
   of Fortune's fatal turn,
may soon in Death's cold silence lie
   'neath some neglected urn.
And none perhaps shall sing my dirge,
   let fall a tear, or mourn
the simple bard who loved so well
   and weeps o'er Balnavoran.

   Patrick Reilly
   from *The Rural Harp*, Drogheda, 1861

ALONG THE BOYNE

you went ahead
your path bruising gently
into the entanglement of grasses that
fume of blossoming weeds nettles daisies
and one bloodred poppy skirted
by the narrow track
while down to the right the weired river
relaxed – like the grass agagain*
(hiding as always its salmon)
to slow forever over curving
into foam rhythms
I followed on that way secret
and delicate as the circles by the reeds

until you were there below
turning smiling in the flowered gown
nettle-burned thumb still to your lips
waiting   where the path stopped

June 1972

        Desmond Egan
    from *Collected Poems*, Goldsmith Press, 1984

* *sic*

31

A ROYAL VISIT

Tara, though she be desolate to-day,
Once was the habitation of heroes ...

from *The Book of Leinster*

I

The deep cooing of doves
as we move toward the earthen fort
is a subtly insidious music
designed to exhort:
axehead of the intellect washed
in hovering fragrance of hawthorn,
the primary colours of a summer morning.

II

This martial extravagance of mounds
cannot be approached simply:
through ritual sagas it resounds
with din of war and love.
Devious virgins and fisty men
gesturing against the sky,
invoke the seasonal crucifixion.

III

Gaelic Acropolis or smoky hovel?
In the enormous osiered banquet hall,
the sotted bards rehearse
a genealogical glory:
stately assonance of verse
petrifies wolf-skinned warriors
in galleries of race.

IV

Who longs for subtler singing,
muted vocal of the dove,
seeks erotic terror ringing
over stony beds of love:
couple and landscape blended,
till beneath the hunchback mountain
plunges the boar of death.

V

A battle of miracles
proves the Christian dispensation,
druidic snow turning
to merciful Christian rain:
Christ is the greater magician.
No more the phallic stone
screams for its ritual king.

VI

A mournful St. Patrick surveys
this provincial magnificence;
he sees what twitching sentries saw
when five regal roads
across a landscape drew:
the central lands of Meath dissolve
into royal planes of blue.

John Montague
from *Poisoned Lands*, The Dolmen Press, 1977

NOT YET BEGUN

The grass held home of the sun all day.
No sound except a bird moping
in the trees' frontier of shadows.
Over there is the road. Cars stray
down it sometimes and the sound goes
away and the boy stops hoping.

Open cries of summer air the air
and then a cloud drifts by. A breeze
darkens out of it and light flies
down the laneway. There's nothing there,
so he goes in, feeling cold seas
the winds blow through and colder skies.

Not knowing why he opens the door
that's closed for strangers, the parlour.
The dust lies waiting on the plush
red seats of the bent-kneed armchairs
but then it rises like a guest
and slows and wanders in the sun.

The boy feels a weight in his chest
of years that are past not yet begun.

Ballivor, Co. Meath

Brian Lynch
from *Beds of Down*, Raven Arts Press, 1983

'Mixer' Dixon went to England
but 'Stonewall' stayed at home.
'The Pope' lived in the Central Bar
and not in holy Rome.

'The Major' Brown lived in our town.
His brother was 'The Jeezer' Jack,
and 'The Whirley' Reilly met a German spy
who fell out of the sky in Glack.

We had in all three Tom Doyles –
a 'Black', a 'White' and a 'Red' or Rua,
and Mr. L'Estrange of Les Boco Stores
was just 'Jabok' to me and you.

'Nanto' Cunningham wed the 'Foxy' Ryan
and they lived up Muchwood Way
while 'The Cruice' Owens raised his glass
and roared 'Up Drumlargan, sin é!'

'The Pinkeen' Dargan ran a sizeable farm.
'The Darkie' Miggin drove a hackney car.
'The Twinny' Byrne gave Fox's Mints to Christian and to
pagan,
'O 'tis sir, 'tis sir, 'tis sir', said 'The Tissir' Fagan.

'Ginger' Owens had jet-black hair
while 'the Towney' Fagan had a London air.
'Spider' Kelly to the GAA was true
and 'the Giant' Dunne was five feet two.

'Sugarstick' Garry was as nice as pie
while 'Arugah!' was Tom Crosby's cry.
'The Bowler' Reynolds hit sixes and fours
and 'Jaykers' McLaughlin ran the General Stores.

'The Showman' Kelly had quite a swagger.
'The Farmer' McKeown was a turnip-snagger.
Christy Fleming hurled as sweet as a fiddle
but why was he called 'Jam in the Middle'?

'Crash' Corrigan had one hour of football glory
and 'What's the News' Leech was on the story.
'The Geanc' Dempsey's nose was truncated
and guess where Dick 'Minaulty' originated?

'The Skipper' Quinn enforced the law of the land
and 'Tar-barrels' Kearney was his next-in-command.
But stand aside 'Skippers' and 'Tar-barrels',
'The Big Man' in town was Fr. Patrick Farrell.

    John Quinn
    from *Goodnight Ballivor, I'll Sleep in Trim*, Veritas, 2008

BELLEWSTOWN RACES

a street ballad

If a respite ye'd borrow from turmoil or sorrow,
    I'll tell ye the secret of how it is done;
'tis found in this version of all the diversion
    that Bellewstown knows when the races comes on.
Make one of a party whose spirits are hearty,
    get a seat on a trap that is safe not to spill,
in its well pack a hamper, then off for a scamper,
    and hurrah for the glories of Bellewstown Hill!

On the road how they rush on – rank, beauty, and fashion!
    It Banagher bangs by the table o' war;
from the coach of the quality, down to the jollity
    jogging along on an ould low-backed car.
Though straw cushions are placed, two feet thick at laste,
    it's concussive jollity to mollify still;
O, the cheeks of my Nelly are shaking like jelly
    from the jolting she gets as she jogs to the Hill.

Arrived at its summit the view that you come at,
    from etherealised Mourne to where Tara ascends,
there's no scene in our sireland – dear Ireland, old Ireland! -
    to which nature more exquisite loveliness lends.
And the soil 'neath your feet has a memory sweet,
    the patriots' deeds they hallow it still;
eighty-two's volunteers (would today saw their peers!)
    marched past in review upon Bellewstown Hill.

But hark! There's a shout, – the horses are out, –
    'long the ropes, on the stand, what a hullaballoo!
To old *Crock-a-Fotha*, the people that dot the
    broad plateau around are all for a view.
"Come, Ned, my tight fellow, I'll bet on the yellow!"
    "Success to the green! Faith, we'll stand by it still!"

The uplands and hollows they're skimming like swallows,
   till they flash by the post upon Bellewstown Hill.

In the tents play the pipers, the fiddlers and fifers,
   those rollicking lilts such as Ireland best knows;
while Paddy is prancing, his colleen is dancing,
   demure, with her eyes quite intent on his toes.
More power to you, Mickey! Faith, your foot isn't sticky,
   but bounds from the boards like a pay from the quill.
O, 'twould cure a rheumatic, - he'd jump up ecstatic
   at "Tatter Jack Walsh" upon Bellewstown Hill.

O, 'tis 'neath the haycocks, all splendid like paycocks,
   in chattering groups that the quality dine;
sitting cross-legged like tailors the gentlemen dealers
   in flattery spout and come out mighty fine.
And the gentry around from Navan and Cavan are "having",
   'neath the shade of the trees, an exquisite quadrille.
All we read in the pages of pastoral ages
   tell of no scene like this upon Bellewstown Hill.

   Anonymous
   from *The Poets and Poetry of Ireland*
   edited by Alfred M. Williams, Osgood, 1881

THE FORT OF BREAKEY

One evening as I rang'd for to recreate my mind
down by the Fort of Breakey to rest I was inclin'd.
I heard two lovers talking; the fair one she did say,
"I pray, young man, don't tease me. Begone, begone away."

He says, *"My charming creature, your favours I implore.*
There is no other female but you I do adore.
Your beauty has enslav'd me. In Cupid's chains I moan.
I am lost in desperation if you do me disown."

Lass:
"I heard my mamma saying when she was brisk and young
that often she experienced young men's deluding tongue.
If you'd meet some other female that might engage your eye,
your vows and protestations of me you would deny."

Lad:
"Your vain imaginations are false I do protest.
'Tis in your fragrant bosom my heart securely rests.
Your curling locks like amber and your teeth like ivory;
from your eyes come killing glances which have entangled me."

With his false persuasion, of her he gained his will,
whilst I lay in concealment beneath the bushes still.
The prayer being twice repeated, the young man went his way
although she did entreat him to wait 'til break of day.

Out of my close concealment to her I did appear.
I asked her the reason she being benighted there.
She says, *"Young fellow, be easy. Don't make of me your game.*
My sins I fear are manifold and here I came to pray."

*"If here to pray you came, I hope you pray'd just right
'The Angelical Salutation' twice on your knees this night."
"I humbly supplicate you to keep this privately."*
He says, *"My dear, you need not fear. No-one shall hear from me."*

Come all ye pretty fair maids who wishes to be kind,
go to the Fort of Breakey where you'll get ease of mind.
Be always very cautious when Paul is passing by
or your tricks he will reveal them if he does you espy.

Rev. Paul O'Brien

from *Gallegan* mss. G1152, National Library of Ireland,
reprinted in *Ríocht na Midhe*, X, 1999

Let Me Come Inland Always

Let me come inland always
to the uneventful plains
where cattle break a pathway
through the slender rains.

Let me come inland always
where beeches freely scatter
green light dappled deeper
where the leaves are doubled.

Let me come inland always
where every wind that passes
tries in vain to rob the grasses
of their green philosophy.

Let me come inland always
where spring hedges hold the rose
and down the wildly tossing fields
the hawthorn galleon blows.

Let me come inland always
where the silence is so great
the lonely bark of the farmer's dog
can deckle edge the night.

Let me come inland always
where you can hardly notice
Time winding his windlass
and only the trees grow old.

Let me come inland always
for fear that I should see
the gold sand shore that brings
such thoughts of the past to me.

I fear those long blonde beaches
as I fear the shores of the past
lest looking down their reaches
I should see with slanted mast
the keeled up happiness of days
that once sailed free.

Mary Lavin
from *Concord of Harps: An Irish P.E.N.*
Anthology of Poetry, The Talbot Press, 1952

THE RACE FIELD

September 11th, 2008

*

A *Transit* towing a load of furlong markers
whose tracks, the farther it goes, grow fainter.

*

A tractor and a harrow preparing sand
to plant and harvest before the tide turns.

*

On the Race Field gate, that lovely extra *s* –
mulled over and gone with - in *Horses Boxes*.

*

Punters eyeing the horizon, like fishermen;
the fishermen, fishing offshore, study form.

*

Neck and neck on the straight for home,
our hands touch; they have lives of their own.

*

No wind; or no wind worth mentioning;
and still the VIP marquee billowing.

*

He drives the final furlong and digs a hole
that the sea fills, for the final furlong pole.

Tom French
from *The Fire Step*, The Gallery Press, 2009

On Seeing Swift in Laracor

I saw them walk that lane again
    and watch the midges cloud a pool,
laughing at something in the brain –
    the Dean and Patrick Brell the fool.

Like Lear he kept his fool with him
    long into Dublin's afterglow,
until the wits in him grew dim
    and Patrick sold him for a show.

Here were the days before Night came,
    when Stella and the other – "slut",
Vanessa, called by him – that flame
    when Laracor was Lilliput!

And here, by walking up and down,
    he made a man called Gulliver,
while bits of lads came out of town
    to have a squint at him and her.

Still, was it Stella that they saw,
    or else some lassie of their own?
For in his story, that's the flaw,
    the secret no one since has known.

Was it some wench among the corn
    has set him from the other two,
some tenderness that he had torn,
    some lovely blossom that he knew?

For when Vanessa died of love,
    and Stella learned to keep her place,
his Dublin soon the story wove
    that steeped them in the Dean's disgrace.

They did not know, 'twas he could tell!
  the reason of his wildest rages,
the story kept by Patrick Brell,
  the thing that put him with the ages.

Now when they mention of the Dean
  some silence holds them as they talk;
some things there are unsaid, unseen,
  that drive me to this lonely walk,

to meet the mighty man again,
  and yet no comfort comes to me.
Although sometimes I see him plain,
  that silence holds the Hill of Bree.

For, though I think I'd know her well,
  I've never seen her on his arm,
laughing with him, nor heard her tell
  she had forgiven all that harm.

And yet I'd like to know 'twere true,
  that here at last in Laracor,
here in the memory of a few,
  there was this rest for him and her.

    Brinsley Mac Namara
    from *Poems of Ireland*, The Irish Times, 1944

St. Patrick's Day

No wise man ever wished to be younger.
                                   Swift

I

Down the long library each marble bust
shines unregarded through a shower of dust
where a grim ghost paces for exercise
in wet weather: nausea, gout, 'some days
I hardly think it worth my time to rise.'
Not even the love of friends can quite appease
the vertigo, sore ears and inner voices;
deep-drafted rain clouds, a rock lost in space,
yahoos triumphant in the market-place,
the isle is full of intolerable noises.

II

Go with the flow; no, going against the grain
he sits in his rocking chair with a migraine,
a light in the church all day till evensong,
the sort of day in which a man might hang.
No riding out to bubbling stream and weir,
to the moist meadow and white belvedere;
on tattling club and coffee-house a pox,
a confederacy of dunces and mohocks –
scholars and saints be d-mn'd, slaves to a hard
reign and our own miniature self-regard.

III

We emerge from hibernation to ghetto-blasters
much better than our old Sony transistors,
consensual media, permanent celebration,
share options, electronic animation,
wave motion of site-specific daffodils
and video lenses in the new hotels;

for Niamh and Oisín have come to earth once more
will blinding breastplate and tempestuous hair,
new festive orthodoxy and ironic icon,
their faces lit up like the Book of Kells.

IV

Defrosting the goose-skin on Bridget's daughters
spring sunlight sparkles among parking meters,
wizards on stilts, witches on circus bikes,
jokers and jugglers, twitching plastic snakes,
pop music of what happens, throbbing skies,
star wars, designer genes, sword sorceries;
we've no nostalgia for the patristic croziers,
fridges and tumble-driers of former years,
rain-spattered cameras in O'Connell St.,
the sound mikes buffeted by wind and sleet –

V

but this is your birthday and I want to recall
a first-floor balcony under a shower of hail
where our own rowdy crowd stood to review
post-Christian gays cavorting up 5th Avenue,
wise-cracking dialogue as quick and dry
as that in *The Big Sleep* or *The Long Goodbye*;
for we too had our seasons in Tír na nÓg,
a Sacred Heart girl and a Protestant rogue,
chill sunshine warming us to the very bone,
our whole existence one erogenous zone.

VI

… A vast opaque body obscured the sun,
rising and falling in an oblique direction,

bright from the sea below, one even plate
above the clouds and vapours, smooth and flat,
adorned with figures of the moon and stars,
fiddles and flutes, the music of the spheres.
The king can deprive them of the dews and rains,
afflicting them with drought and diseases;
or drop stones, against which no defence,
directly upon their heads whenever he pleases ...

VII

Borneo, Japan; night breezes, and while they breathe
hawthorn and bluebell of Armagh and Meath
a mouse watches where, beside confining quays
in a dirty-windowed website computer loft,
brain circuits off in the dark hovercraft,
he inhales the helium of future centuries,
the new age of executive science fiction,
flying islands in focus, no lateral vision,
the entire universe known, owned and reified
except for a tiny glitch that says to hide.

VIII

I now resign these structures and devices,
these fancy flourishes and funny voices
to a post-literate, audio-visual realm
of uncial fluorescence, song and film,
as curious symptoms of a weird transition
before we opted to be slaves of fashion
– for now, whatever our ancestral dream,
we give ourselves to a vast corporate scheme
where our true wit is devalued once again,
our solitude remembered by the rain.

IX

The one reality is the perpetual flow,
chaos of complex systems; each generation
does what it must; middle age and misanthropy,
like famine and religion, make poor copy;
and even the present vanishes like snow
off a rope, frost off a ditch, ice in the sun –
so back to the desk-top and the drawing board,
prismatic natural light, slow-moving cloud,
the waves far-thundering in a life of their own,
a young woman hitching a lift on a country road.

Derek Mahon
from *Collected Poems*, The Gallery Press, 1999

IOMÁIN NA BÓINNE

(The Boyne v. The Nanny, c.1700)

Ba aigeantach croíúil mo mhachnamh ag teach aníos
ar an ochtú lá fichead d'*October*,
is dá mbeinnse lean dtaoibh b'fhogas dóibh fíon
ina chasc a fháil ón rí tráthnóna.
Beidh cuimhne ag síogaí na hAnaí go síorraí
ar mo churaí nár claíodh lena bpónair,
is go raibh an bála ag dul tríofu mar ealta le gaoith
ag seabhaic ghlana líofa na Bóinne.

Tháinig síol Uidhir séanmhar de laochraí Loch Éirne,
nach gcloífí le céadtaí, ár dtarrtháil;
agust trí mic in éineacht d'fhíorfhuil na Raghallach
ina suí go ró-spéiriúil sa mbáire;
faoiteach na féile a bhfuil mianach na nGael ann –
'sé rí-mharcach réimiúil na bpátrún,
agus Séamus mo thréanfhear Ó hÉinigh le héifeacht
ag scaoileadh is ag réabadh lucht prácais;

tháinig Mac Cléirigh óg ann a leagfadh na sluaite
mar Shamson ag stróiceadh na leomhan
nó mar Hercules i gcomhrac le fathach na Cremona,
nó mar Hector nó Troilus i gnuasacht;
mar Chadmus ag stróiceadh na ndragan le crógacht,
nó Atlas an eolais in uaigneas –
is mar sin a bhí Seoirse agus macraidh na Bóinne
ag cur balla ar lucht próib agus uafáis.

'Siad seabhaic Bhaile Shláine na curaí is áille,
ariamh nár thuill náire don uaisle –
a bhrisfeadh gach sárbhuíon dá gcruinneochadh le báire
ina gceann gan chairde na huaire.
B'aoibhinn an lá sin bheith i bhFionnabhair ar na hardaí
ag amharc ar rásaí na mbuachall,

is níl ríon den Ádhamhchlainn a chífeadh mo pháistí
nach líonfadh i ngrá leo an uair sin!

Más bead libh a bhfuair sibh i bhFionnabhair an uair sin
de imirt ag buachaillí Bóinne,
cruinnigí bhur sluaite fán Anaidh le buabhall
ó Theamhair go cuan Bhaile Uí Mhornáin –
tugadh taispeánadh uathu, más toil leo an bualadh,
is bíodh an tAilíneach leo suas fá Fheil Iósaif,
beidh mo mhacnaidhse in uachtar á gcarnadh ina gcruachaí
chun an Mhuilinn ar cuairt chun na Róistí!

Séamus Dall Mac Cuarta (c. 1650–1732/3)

MIDDLE KINGDOM

Middle kingdom, where you are
is where the deepest, most arcane
dwellings of the senses are.
History is your wall of pain.

Garrison, the planter's warp
in the rebel climate's grain,
sleep-fortress, wall of class and sex,
beset by dream, besought by blame.

The masters of the middle kingdom
where centuries slip out in a sigh,
where time has bred into language,
are conspiring at last to fly

beyond the codes they have mastered,
beyond their system-built walls.
Besieged and besiegers are tasting
truth's vinegar, treason, heart's gall.

Seamus Deane
from *Selected Poems,* The Gallery Press, 1988

An Irish Requiem

i.m. Mary Lynch (1897–1983), Windtown, Navan

Born in another country, under a different flag
She did not die before her time
Her god never ceased to speak to her.
And so she did not die. The only death that is real
Is when words change their meaning
And that is a death she never knew
Born in another country, under a different flag
When the soldiers and armoured cars
Spilled out of the ballads and onto the screen
Filling the tiny streets, she cried
And wiped her eyes on her apron, mumbling something
About the Troubles. That was a word
I had learned in my history book.
What did I care for the wails of the balding Orpheus
As he watched Eurydice burn in hell?
I was eleven years old,
And my Taoiseach wrote to me,
Born in another country, under a different flag.
She did not die before her time
She went without fuss, into the grave
She had bought and tended herself, with
The priest to say rites at her entry
And the whole family gathered,
Black suits and whiskey, a cortège
Of Ford Avengers inching up the cemetery hill.
Death came as an unexpected visitor,
A policeman, or rate collector, or the tinker
Who called every spring for fresh eggs,
Announced by the season, or knocks on walls,
Bats flying in and out of rooms, to signify
She did not die before her time
Her god never ceased to speak to her.
Till the last, he murmured in her kitchen

As she knelt at the chair beside the range
Or moved to the damp, unused parlour
For the priest's annual visit.
Poète de sept ans, I sat on the polished wood,
Bored by the priest's vernacular harangue
As she knelt beside me on the stone church floor,
And overheard her passionate whisper,
Oblivious, telling her beads, and I knew
That I would remember this, that
Her god never ceased to speak to her.
As so she did not die. The only death that is real
Is when words change their meaning
And that is a death she never knew.
As governments rose and fell, she never doubted
The name of the land she stood on. Nothing
But work and weather darkened the spring days
When she herded her fattened cattle
Onto the waiting cars. It is not she who haunts
But I, milking her life for historical ironies,
Knowing that more than time divides us.
But still her life burns on, like the light
From a distant, extinguished star, and
O let me die before that light goes out
Born in another country, under a different flag!

Michael O'Loughlin
from *Another Nation: New and Selected Poems*,
New Island, 1996

LOUGHCREW

They say, I've always heard,
there's not a lake in County Meath.
The width or breadth of it
no river swells or springs collect.
I'm living in the townland of Loughcrew,
loch na craoibhe, lake of the limb
of the oak on the island.

I wasn't born here but I came
to be at home near my home place.
I'm looking at the maps
and see the lake, a boat-house,
trees in Traynors' field,
a pair of islands. Now there's one.

They say that I say little,
say I fish in deeper waters.
An island is lost, a lake is found
and I translate an early verse:
'*I am the poor hag of Bera.*
Many a wonder have I seen.
I have seen Carnbawn a lake
although it's now a mountain green.'

      Peter Fallon
      from *Winter Work*, The Gallery Press, 1983

The Burial of King Cormac

'Crom Cruach and his sub-gods twelve,'
    said Cormac, 'are but carven treene;
the axe that made them, haft or helve,
    had worthier of our worship been.

'But He who made the tree to grow,
    and hid in earth the iron-stone,
and made the man with mind to know
    the axe's use, is God alone.'

Anon to priests of Crom was brought –
    where, girded in their service dread,
they minister'd on red Moy Slaught –
    word of the words King Cormac said.

They loosed their curse against the king;
    they cursed him in his flesh and bones;
and daily in their mystic ring
    they turn'd the maledictive stones,

till, where at meat the monarch sate,
    amid the revel and the wine,
he choked upon the food he ate,
    at Sletty, southward of the Boyne.

High vaunted then the priestly throng,
    and far and wide they noised abroad
with trump and loud liturgic song
    the praise of their avenging God.

But 'ere the voice was wholly spent
    that priest and prince should still obey,
to awed attendants o'er him bent
    great Cormac gather'd breath to say, –

'Spread not the beds of Brugh for me
    when restless death-bed's use is done:
But bury me at Rossnaree
    and face me to the rising sun.

'For all the kings who lie in Brugh
    put trust in gods of wood and stone;
and 'twas at Ross that first I knew
    One, Unseen, who is God alone.

'His glory lightens from the east;
    his message soon shall reach our shore;
and idol-god, and cursing priest
    shall plague us from Moy Slaught no more.'

Dead Cormac on his bier they laid:-
    'He reign'd a king for forty years,
and shame it were,' his captains said,
    'He lay not with his royal peers.

'His grandsire, Hundred-Battle, sleeps
    serene in Brugh: and, all around,
dead kings in stone sepulchral keeps
    protect the sacred burial ground.

'What though a dying man should rave
    of changes o'er the eastern sea?
In Brugh of Boyne shall be his grave,
    and not in noteless Rossnaree.'

Then northward forth they bore the bier,
    and down from Sletty side they drew,
with horsemen and with charioteer,
    to cross the fords of Boyne to Brugh.

There came a breath of finer air
    that touch'd the Boyne with ruffling wings,
it stirr'd him in his sedgy lair
    and in his mossy moorland springs.

And as the burial train came down
    with dirge and savage dolorous shows,
across their pathway, broad and brown,
    the deep, full-hearted river rose;

from bank to bank through all his fords,
    'neath blackening squalls he swell'd and boil'd;
and thrice the wondering gentile lords
    essay'd to cross, and thrice recoil'd.

Then forth stepp'd grey-hair'd warriors four:
    they said, *'Through angrier floods than these,*
on link'd shields once our king we bore
    from Dread-Spear and the hosts of Deece.

'And long as loyal will holds good,
    and limbs respond with helpful thews,
nor flood, nor fiend within the flood,
    shall bar him of his burial dues.'

With slanted necks they stoop'd to lift;
    they heaved him up to neck and chin;
and, pair and pair, with footsteps swift,
    lock'd arm and shoulder, bore him in.

'Twas brave to see them leave the shore;
    to mark the deep'ning surges rise,
and fall subdued in foam before
    the tension of their striding thighs.

'Twas brave, when now a spear-cast out,
    breast-high the battling surges ran;
for weight was great, and limbs were stout,
    and loyal man put trust in man.

But 'ere they reach'd the middle deep,
    nor steadying weight of clay they bore,
nor strain of sinewy limbs could keep
    their feet beneath the swerving four.

And now they slide, and now they swim,
    and now, amid the blackening squall,
grey locks afloat, with clutching grim,
    they plunge around the floating pall.

While, as a youth with practised spear
    through justling crowds bears off the ring,
Boyne from their shoulders caught the bier
    and proudly bore away the king.

At morning, on the grassy marge
    of Rossnaree, the corpse was found,
and shepherds at their early charge
    entomb'd it in the peaceful ground.

A tranquil spot: a hopeful sound
    comes from the ever youthful stream,
and still on daisied mead and mound
    the dawn delays with tenderer beam.

Round Cormac Spring renews her buds:
    In march perpetual by his side,
down come the earth-fresh April floods
    and up the sea-fresh salmon glide;

and life and time rejoicing run
    from age to age their wonted way;
but still he waits the risen Sun,
    for still 'tis only dawning Day.

Samuel Ferguson
from *The Poems of Samuel Ferguson*, edited by Padraic Colum,
Allen Figgis, 1963

A Day with the Meaths

I drove through Dunshaughlin, straight on for Clonee,
had a dentist appointment in Dublin at three;
met a mud-spattered horse which a groom slowly led,
a hound van I recognised farther ahead
by its number plate (Meath thirty-six-sixty-three);
then, rounding a bend, was delighted to see
gay scarlet a-bob in a lane to my right,
hounds coming from Batterstown – glorious sight!
Tossed a coin. Head for dentist. And heads won the toss;
but I turned after hounds at the Ten-Mile-Bush cross!
(where Collier the Robber rode) reached Hanley's Lane.
Then followed the car stream to see hounds again.
Passing Fairyhouse Racecourse I saw them once more
taking short-cut to covert across Big Lagore.
Reaching Navan-Ratoath road, a left-handed wheel
brought me past Thunder's Wood. Soon I saw a Whip steal
very quietly round to a gate at the wood
called Little Lagore. There he silently stood
while hounds were put in ….pack had plenty to say!
Mr. Fox didn't argue! He just slipped away.
Though the statuesque Whipper-in witnessed him go,
he gave plenty of law 'ere he yelled *"Tally-ho!"*
From wood to house-laurels hounds dashed, speaking true,
then across Thunder's Lawn. Such a marvellous view!

Three o'clock! Mr. Dentist, your drill is a bore;
who'd swop anaesthetics for hounds at Lagore?

Stanislaus Lynch
from *Rhymes of an Irish Huntsman*, County Life, 1937

A DREAM OF SOLSTICE

Qual e colui che sognando vede,
che dopo 'l sogno la passione impressa
rimane, e l'altro a la mente non riede,

cotal son io...
        Dante, *Paradiso*, Canto xxxiii

Like somebody who sees things when he's dreaming
and after the dream lives with the aftermath
of what he felt, no other trace remaining,

so I live now, for what I saw departs
and is almost lost, although a distilled sweetness
still drops from it into my inner heart.

It is the same with snow the sun releases,
the same as when in wind, the hurried leaves
swirl round your ankles and the shaking hedges

that had flopped their catkin cuff-lace and green sleeves
are sleet-whipped bare. Dawn light began stealing
through the cold universe to county Meath,

over weirs where the river Boyne goes curling
imperturbably, over standing stones
millennia deep in their own unmoving

and unmoved alignment. And now the planet turns
its clay-cold brow as a watching crowd stands still
in the wired-off precinct of the burial mounds,

Flight 104 from New York audible
as it descends on schedule into Dublin,
the car park silent, the assembled people

waiting for seedling light on roof and windscreen,
for the addled sun to riddle through the murk
and overboiling cloud, for a milted glow

and eastern dazzle
to send first light like share-shine in a furrow
steadily deeper, farther available,

creeping along the floor of the passage grave
to backstone and capstone, holding its candle
to the world inside the astronomic cave.

Seamus Heaney

AN OLD BOYNE FISH BARN

You should have seen the sea in those days,
wind smoke and weeping flares washing

ashore from the barrios, all those
hesitant evacuees, as tarpaulin stretched

along Beaufort's Dyke and our drift nets
sailed through the Hebrides. Shuffling in pipe

smoke, scribbling a plume of grave longing
on the bones of a wax-bright dusk,

I stood to see the ranks at the fish barn –
open mouthed, open boxed, iced on shelf

after shelf – and stayed to inhabit
what remains for the solipsistic raconteur

who believes the weight of his vision
will dissolve with the last sight. When I drag

a heavy catch out of the evening,
old weather, braced for meteorites,

groans like a dehumidifier and burbles
the gospel of faith and love and water.

      Gerard Fanning

O'Carolan's Complaint

The great tunes
I never played are lost
to monied patronage, the lit rooms
in grey façades

whisper, fall silent
at their harmony and grace. I think
of all the girls I might have loved
instead of music –

one hand finding melody
as easily as the pulse of a heart,
the other making fluent gestures
towards the purse of love.

My real performances
never yet embraced an actual beauty –
mere competence, my inward ear
and theirs heard better:

like intervals of silence
between the notes,
their upturned faces wanting more,
the lives I never lived.

Ciarán Carson
from *The New Estate*, The Gallery Press, 1988

The Bridge of Clonee (1856)

Tune: "Tally-ho! says the Squire, with a terrible roar."

This song was presented to Samuel Reynell, Esq., Master of the Hounds, with the painting by Baldock, given him by the Members of the Hunt.

From the Bridge of Clonee to the banks of Loughsheelin
lies Maghbreagh which in summer's a sweet place to dwell in;
from old Ballyboggin to Bettystown strand,
So green and refreshing 'tis the pride of Ireland;
    with its cattle and sheep, dozing to sleep
    on a fine summer's day amid oceans of keep.

But when Autumn's first frosts on the leaves mark their stain,
oh! what mists would envelop that beautiful plain.
When October's short days close in, gloomy and black,
if 'twere not for Sam Reynell and his famous pack;
    with Martin and Cox hunting their fox,
    their music quite melting the hearts in the rocks.

Then the glen of Kilmainham and Whitewood resound
to his cry of *"Hark, for'ard!"*, to cheer the young hound;
and at Kingsfort and Summerville, Slane and Muchwood,
he scatters the foxes and gives his hounds blood.
    "Hark, for'ard!" his cry, "never say die.
    Stay with me, I'll show you good sport by-and-by."

With dreary November his first list appears,
when we all flock to meet him and join in his cheers.
To old Allenstown, Bengerstown, Killallon gorse,
where he well tests the mettle of hound, man and horse.
    Still "Hark, for'ard!" his cry. "Never say die.
    Stay with me. I'll show you good sport by-and-by."

So in blustry December, what care we for weather?
We ne'er mope at home, for he brings us together.
And there's many a good thing then marked on each card
from sweet Rathmanoe, Coolestown and Tullyard.
    Still *"Hark, for'ard!"* his cry. *"Never say die.*
    Stay with me. I'll show you good sport by-and-by."

A Meet at Dunboyne brings the Dublin men out,
in the morning they're bumptious and ride very stout;
but an evening old fox from Culmullen hill
makes them sing out *"peccavi"* and gives them their fill.
    Down dale and up hill, by Clavanstown Mill –
    Oh! wirrastrue! Sure their horses they kill.

When old Christmas comes round and good cheer most abounds,
how he brightens the place with the jolly Meath hounds.
When the boys come from school and the girls have their Ball
at Balrath, Loughcrew, Headfort and Corbalton Hall;
when they meet, great and small, boys, girls and all,
and every man's house is chuck-full for the Ball.

Old Mountainstown then is a favourite Meet
where this hearty good fellow gets often a treat;
and well he deserves all that Meath-men can give
for without him in winter 'twere a dull place to live.
For no balls we should have, nor dinners we'd give
if we had not Sam Reynell to keep us alive.

As the spring opens up, the real clipping begins
and many an old fox now dies in his sins;
but to mention each run in the bounds of this song
would but spoil our diversion and make it too long;
for, though it may have merit, I know you'd declare it
a very great bore if it kept back the claret.

His men, hounds and horses are the best of good stuff
and there's no man can say there's not hunting enough.
So let's fill up our glasses and give us three rounds
of the 'crow-bar' to Reynell and his jolly hounds.
And long may he reign o'er the beautiful plain,
for we never shall have such a master again.

Anonymous
from *Verses and Rhymes of the Meath Hunt*, n.d.

MAGH BREAGH

O River
of god-given kings and king's offspring,
of agile water craft and gleaming salmon;
O Boyne, host to the games and hard battles,
and to heroes of the Royal Race of Conn!
O sorrowed Boyne! O stream of many tears!

Padraic Gregory
after the eighteenth century Irish

COME GATHER ROUND ME PARNELLITES

Come gather round me Parnellites
and praise our chosen man,
stand upright on your legs awhile,
stand upright while you can,
for soon we lie where he is laid
and he is underground;
come fill up all those glasses
and pass the bottle round.

And here's a cogent reason
and I have many more,
he fought the might of England
and saved the Irish poor,
whatever good a farmer's got
he brought it all to pass;
and here's another reason,
that Parnell loved a lass.

And here's a final reason,
he was of such a kind
every man that sings a song
keeps Parnell in his mind
for Parnell was a proud man,
no prouder trod the ground,
and a proud man's a lovely man
so pass the bottle round.

The Bishops and the Party
that tragic story made,
a husband that had sold his wife
and after that betrayed;
but stories that live longest
are sung above the glass,
and Parnell loved his country
and Parnell loved his lass.

William Butler Yeats
from *New Poems*, 1937

In Memoriam – F.R. Higgins

When we saw the moss-scented earth of your loved Meath
    cover you,
hap you in from the chill of that wintry morn,
not death was in the thought of those who bowed over you,
but life, and life abundant, from which are born
brimmed beakers, and laughter unfettered, and brave
    uncensored song.
'*Earth to earth*', but earth kindly, triumphant, unmourning.
As of old the laughter-lit waves by the Sirmian headland
lapped round the barque, in glee at their poet's returning
so the loved light earth of your Laracor welcomed you home.

    Seumas O'Sullivan
    from *This is the House and Other Verses*, O'Sullivan, 1942

AFTER THE SLANE CONCERT: BASTILLE DAY 1987

The dark girl drinking cider in the bar
smiles speaking of her knife
my ears prick at the hint of violence
with thoughts of a dark street in Paris
almost thirty years ago
stoned high and fighting with a one-eyed Arab
above that Metro shelter
the quick flash of violence and sex
and short knives stabbing across the street

He was pissing sideways says the girl
like he wasn't aiming straight
and... and here her voice drops out of sight
her hair mingles with her neighbour's
like curtains falling across the street
I think of Borges' Argentinians
dying in limelight under street lamps
it is all so casual so promiscuous
so soft these lethal beautiful parishioners

And was it really just like this –
an inner city pub where careless Fates
blast on cider and cigarettes
so sure footed and so self-contained
so dangerous
the smile that seems as innocent of violence
as the knife-blade in its hidden place
and one maimed look is all it needs
to make us human
reading in the morning ash for messages of love

Macdara Woods
from *Selected Poems*, Dedalus Press, 1996

'LAST SONGS' BY FRANCIS LEDWIDGE

I hold this book you have never seen,
published by Herbert Jenkins, London,
in the armistice of nineteen eighteen,

before those of your limbs they could salvage
were re-buried in grave number 5, row B,
The Second Plot, Artillery Wood Cemetery.

When I was younger you were like a brother,
at night I wanted your ghost to haunt me.

Now, reading you again, what I most reject
are the faults I abhor in my younger self.

We have so little left in common, Frank:
Yet I know when it comes my turn
to venture down the tunnel of the unknown

you will be among the hallucinogenic ranks
of shuffled faces crowding in to welcome.
Finally we shall recognise each other.

1996

Dermot Bolger
from *Taking My Letters Back*, New Island Books, 1998

THE RAM

As I went down through Clonmellon town
it was on a market day
I met the biggest ram, sir,
that ever was fed on hay.

This ram he had four feet, sir,
for him on which to stand,
and every step he took
would cover an acre of land.

Singing: Ho dingle darby and hi dingle dee
Ho dingle darby, tura lura lee.

This ram he had a tail, sir
most wonderful to tell.
It went all round Archerstown
and rang Miss Reynell's bell.

Singing: Ho dingle darby and hi dingle dee
Ho dingle darby, tura lura lee.

This ram, sir, he had a horn
that grew up to the moon.
P____ W_____ went up in February
and didn't come down till June.

Singing: Ho dingle darby and hi dingle dee
Ho dingle darby, tura lura lee.

The man, sir, that killed the ram
was up to his neck in blood;

and the boy that held the basin
was carried away by the flood.

Singing: *Ho dingle darby and hi dingle dee*
                Ho dingle darby, tura lura lee.

Anonymous

AN OBAIR

An móta is bábhún Normannach a chonac isteach thar chuirtín
    crann
is mé ag tiomáint thar bráid go tapaidh ar an mbóthar,
áit éigin faoin dtuath in aice le Cill Mhaighneann
I gContae na Mí, a thugann an ainm don áit. Sin í An Obair.

É sin is an cara mná is ansa liom ar domhan ag fáil bháis go mall
in Oispidéal an Adelaide: an grianghraf thíos im' phóca dínn
    beirt inár mná óga
a tógadh lá Márta, an chéad lá earraigh i nGairdín na mBláth in
    Ankara
na Tuirce, sinn ag gáirí is gan tuairim againn ar cad a bhí
    romhainn;

aghaidh na mná Moslamaí ón Ailgéir a chonac le déanaí sa
    nuachtán
nuair a hinsíodh di go rabhthas tar éis an scornach a ghearradh
ar ochtar leanbh óg dá clann; an file iomráiteach Seirbeach
a bhí ina cheannaire ar mhórchampa géibhinn; an staraí
    litríochta
a chaith a chuid ama saor lena chairde ag imirt caide le plaosc
    dhaonna;

m'fhear céile a chaith sé lá i gcóma is mé ag féachaint amach
    fuinneoga
an tseomra feithimh ar an solas ag dorchú amuigh ar an mbá
idir Dún Laoghaire is Binn Éadair, is ar theacht is imeach na
    taoide;
trácht trom ar an mbóthar mar a raibh an saol Fódlach ag rith
    sall
is anall, ag plódú ar nós na nduilleog a bhí ag péacadh ar gach
    aon chrann;

é seo go léir a thabhairt faoi ndeara is áit a dhéanamh dó id'
    chroí gan pléascadh,

é seo uile is an móta Normannach a chonac is mé ag gabháil na slí,
áit éigin faoin dtuath in aice le Cill Mhaighneann i gContae na Mí,
An Obair. Sin í an obair. Sin í an obair nach éasca.

Nuala Ní Dhomhnaill
from *The Fifty-Minute Mermaid*, The Gallery Press, 2007

THE TASK

It's from the massive Norman earthworks I glimpsed through
        a curtain of trees
as I drove quickly past,
somewhere near Kilmainham, County Meath,
that the place took its name. Nobber. From the Irish *an obair*,
    'the task'.

From that and my dearest friend slowly dying
in the Adelaide Hospital; the photograph deep in my pocket
        of us as young women,
taken on a March day, the first day of spring in the Botanic
        Gardens in Ankara,
laughing, with no sense of what was to come;

the face of the Muslim woman from Algeria I saw in a news-
        paper lately
after she was told lately that the throats
of eight of her children had been cut; the major Serbian poet
who was the commandant of a major camp; the literary
        historian
who enjoyed an off-moment with his friends, playing ball
        with a human skull;

my own husband who spent six days in a coma while I
        looked out the windows
of the waiting room at the light going down on the bay
between Dun Laoghaire and Howth, at the come and go of
        the tide;
heavy traffic on the road as the entire population of Ireland
        rushed here and there,
countless as bud-blasts from the trees;

to take it all in, to make room in your heart without having
        your heart burst,
to take in not only this but that Norman motte and bailey

I passed near Kilmainham or thereabouts,
a place called Nobber. That's the task. *An obair*. A task that's
   far from easy.

(translated by Paul Muldoon)

A WHITE ROSE

The red rose whispers of passion,
   and the white rose breathes of love;
oh, the red rose is a falcon,
   and the white rose is a dove.

But I send you a cream-white rosebud
   with a flush on its petal tips;
for the love that is purest and sweetest
   has a kiss of desire on the lips.

John Boyle O'Reilly
from *In Bohemia*, The Pilot Publishing Co., 1886

Oliver Plunkett

His Soul

When they cut off his head, the long whiskers
went on growing, as if to fledge his soul
and facilitate its gradual departure.

So much of him was concentrated there
that, quite without his realising it,
they divided the body into four.

It amounted to more than a withdrawal
when the last drop of moisture had dispersed
and one by one the hairs fell from his chin,

for the fatty brain was shrivelling as well,
leaving around itself enormous spaces
and accomodation for the likes of him.

His own leathery shine, he seems to be
refracting the gleam in his father's eye
like a shattered mirror in a handbag.

His Head

This is the end of the body that thinks
and says things, says things as the body does –
kisses, belches, sighs – while making room for
the words of wisdom and the testimonies.

And these are a baby's features, a child's
expression condensing on the plate glass,
the specimen suspended in its bottle
at eye level between shelf and shelf.

His head looks out from the tiny coffin
as though his body were crouching there
inside the altar, a magician
who is in charge of this conjuring trick,

or an astronaut trapped by his oxygen
and eager to float upwards to the ceiling
away from the gravitational pull
of his arms and legs which are very old.

Your own face is reflected by the casket
and this is anybody's head in a room
except that the walls are all windows and
he has written his name over the glass.

His Body

Trying to estimate what height he was
keeps the soul awake, like the pea under
the heap of mattresses under the princess.

And now that they've turned him into a saint
even a fly buzzing about the roof space
must affect the balance of his mind.

His thigh bones and shoulder blades are scales
that a speck of dust could tilt, making him
walk with a limp or become a hunchback.

He has been buried under the fingernails
of his executioners, until they too fade
like the lightning flash of their instruments.

There accompanies him around the cathedral
enough silence to register the noise
of the hairs on arms and legs expiring.

Michael Longley
from *The Echo Gate 1975–1979*, Secker & Warburg, 1979

An Smiota

An bhlaosc chrón chríon sa scrín
san eaglais cois na Bóinne
níor bhain an smiota de do bhéal,
ach b'áil liom a fhiafraí
céard a thug tú chun na háite
ó mheasas narbh údar blaosc chun gáire,
is cheapas gur rugadh tú in antráth
is dá mairteá le linn Herod Rí,
go dtabharfá blaosc an Naoimh isteach
is aoibh an gháire ort.

The Smirk

That yellow, dried-up skull in the shrine
in the church beside the Boyne
didn't wipe that smirk from your mouth,
but I wanted to ask
what brought you there
since I judged a skull no cause for laughter,
and I thought to myself you'd been born too late
for if you'd lived when Herod was king,
you would have brought the saint's head in
with a smile on your lips.

Máirtín Ó Direáin
from *Selected Poems*, The Goldsmith Press, 1984

NEWGRANGE

I hear them laughing in their tombs,
the old ones in their house of stone.
Their home is a time-proofed plan
inscrutable as a druid's dream
three open *ushabti* and a single fern
threw cosmology into rune.
Long before Ogham the talking
began and what seems sepulchral
is stone-dream song. What
was chiselled happens continually;
their laughter mocks history –
nothing certain, nothing sacred,
only stones celebrating some mystery.

Lynda Moran
from *The Truth About Lucy*, Beaver Row Press, 1985

BOYNE VALLEY

On a mound chipped
from the dead, deity
and scantlings dismantled, the spell broken,
I stand on a stone ship
that sails nowhere

but once was set right to launch
the bronze and brandished hero, fellow
of this same sun that low now
in bare twigs
lies lumped in the winter's wicker basket,

who was laid in
this hill of metaphor, as if a grave has no end,
suspended in some state of grace above
his own diving depths,
to find North like the barnacle

and a quite definite eternal Paradise
(only the best admitted, Stags
of the year, Gods
in the demi-brackets) not very different from this;
but Paradise is always somewhere else,

leaving his head to the stone axe, and the big, broken
torque of his body to dangle,
wail, ye women,
God is dead
and picked over by this year's summer students,

whose secret name was
a flight of months, the whole earth offering
its barbarous alphabet to make him delicate;
now trees and stone have forgotten; the birds
are entirely without auspices

and preen flit strut in winter attitudes,
birds, not litanies. The thing is gone
now that no giant drops from the gaudy zenith
like Mad Sweeney
to hang on the last Elder tree head and antlers.

Flayed, to be scattered in this the thirteenth
unlucky month, for Fertility, for a patch
of emmer barley, for all men –
to give their guts literally to this, –
to Demeter the first plough.

A sow, snouted with the moon's horn! But
it's Isis I think of, Magna Mater, to whom
the divine members from their schism clambered;
into the magnet they came, the brilliant head
topping the whole winged tread again –

meaning just a new sun
on the old wheel, the one wheel, and world safe inside
the big roll of gravity, but
aware there is a moment
when all things could fall in,

as indeed they may,
for all this peaceful scene, Boyne cease to flow
broad through this green valley with
its copious flood
of ephemeral nature notes,

such as one swaying sunheaded reed,
such as a crow daubed on the ripple of
a black poplar, a thrusting ash
in its hedgeleap carrying
the long horizon on a twig, twice.

Distantly a horn, not Herne and his hounds but
esquires at play, a near hill rolls gold
for some unearthly reason,
and maybe too this battered helmet of a place
I straddle cold

with sheep suddenly on the fosse;
souls? No, merely ewes
and wearing the ram's pigments, the autumn's raddle;
fertility minds its own business;
and world will go on more or less

the same notwithstanding God
or Goddess; only man the danger. Still
it must be heartening in ill times to have
ties with the whole network,
God on the wire inside a hill.

Jaguars roll from the meet, trailing
horseheads and dogfoxes. History
is slowly reaching some conclusion somewhere:
and here is the usual tentative dusk
as day runs out of silver

and one flintnebbed swan owns all the Boyne;
no afterglow or
gold bowl to sail home the antlered one,
surrogate, heraldic sufferer,
Cerumnos, Arthur, Bran.

Padraic Fallon
from *Poems*, The Dolmen Press, 1974

Unwanted Apples

on a wintry bough, blasted
by ice-tipped winds,
a poor man's pie.

If one with gathering pail came,
what uplift to the tree's dignity –
to accept the blessing

and thwart the fear
of life without reason or cause;
a singer with a song to no applause.

Paddy Meegan

THE ECHO GATE

I stand between the pillars of the gate,
a skull between two ears that reconstructs
broken voices, broken stones, history

and the first words that come into my head
echoing back from the monastery wall
to measure these fields at the speed of sound.

Michael Longley
from *The Echo Gate 1975–1979*, Secker & Warburg, 1979

The Song of Mary Cruise

Ah, Blessed Mary! Hear me sighing,
on this cold stone, mean labours plying;
yet Rathmore's heiress might I name me.
And broad lands rich and many claim me.
Gilstown, Rathbeg, names known from childhood;
fair Johnstown, hard by bog and wild wood.
Rathaffe, (Blackwater near it floweth),
and Harton, where the white wheat groweth.
Kilskeer, with windows shining brightly,
Teltown where race the coursers sprightly.
Balreask, abundant dairies showing,
full pails and churns each day bestowing.
Thee, Ballycred, too, memory prizes,
old Oristown to mind arises.
Caultown, near bogs, black turf providing;
Rathkenny, in its 'Baron' priding.
The Twelve Poles, Armabregia follow,
Kilmainham of the woody hollow.
Cruisetown with lake by sunbeams greeted,
Moydorragh gay 'mid fair woods seated.
Still could I speak of townlands many,
three score along the banks of Nanny;
twelve by the Boyne, if it were pleasure
to dwell on lost and plundered treasure.

Anonymous

BLUEBELLS FOR LOVE

There will be bluebells growing under the big trees
and you will be there and I will be there in May;
for some other reason we both will have to delay
the evening in Dunshaughlin – to please
some imagined relation,
so both of us came to walk through that plantation.

We will be interested in the grass,
in an old bucket-hoop, in the ivy that weaves
green incongruity among dead leaves,
we will put on surprise at carts that pass –
only sometimes looking sideways at the bluebells in the
    plantation
and never frighten them with too wild an exclamation.

We will be wise, we will not let them guess
that we are watching them or they will pose
a mere façade like boys
caught out in virtue's naturalness.
We will not impose on the bluebells in that plantation
too much of our desire's adulation.

We will have other loves – or so they'll think;
the primroses or the ferns or the briars,
or even the rusty paling wires,
or the violets on the sunless sorrel bank.
Only as an aside the bluebells in the plantation
will mean a thing to our dark contemplation.

We'll know love little by little, glance by glance.
Ah, the clay under these roots is so brown!

We'll steal from Heaven while God is in the town –
I caught an angel smiling in a chance
look through the tree-trunks of the plantation
as you and I walked slowly to the station.

Patrick Kavanagh
from *A Soul for Sale*, Macmillan, 1947

LÍADAN TELLS OF HER LOVE FOR CUIRITHIR

Unpleasing
the deed I did
what I loved I killed.

Were it not
for fear of Heaven
I'd have risked the Devil.

Not small
what he desired
to avoid fire.

A trifle
vexed him towards me
I loved him greatly.

I am Líadan
Cuirithir I loved
easily proved.

A little while
I was in his company
and it was sweet to me.

Forest music
used to sing to me
and the fierce sea.

I had thought
nothing I could do
would change his view.

Conceal it not
he had my heart
others my art.

A roar of fire
has split this heart of mine
without him I pine.

Now the way she vexed him was her haste in taking the veil.

Donagh MacDonagh
from *A Warning to Conquerors*, The Dolmen Press, 1968

The Hill of Tara Recollected at Locarno

for Salvador de Madariaga

Beyond Howth and the Skerries,
that Hill: the green, the wet, the wind, the cows.
Not garrulous, no Crown of Thorns, nor berries,
non-committal, non-Christian, mnemophogus.

Pearly, teethy voices sing green songs of forgetfulness
of a Queen sitting on a pointed rock like a wind-daft
giantess.

Here, now, beyond the medieval casement of the Castello Visconti
the Socratic *sindaco* stares at the Alp –
a Madonna for every rocky periphery –
and listens to the exile who spurned the cup.

A roaring fire in the walk-in grate and all the red camellias
attest to a Platonic aristocracy in exile, abiding unbanishable laws.

Anthony Kerrigan
from *At The Front Door of the Atlantic*, The Dolmen Press,
1969

BETTYSTOWN

what if before cars and transistors
it was here the winter-sailing Vikings
fell from the horizon, breathless
with misdeeds to do, waded ashore
with bearded cries, clangour of fierce
metal – what strange thwacks did they
deal in the name of our week-days?

a sputter of white low tide where
minuscule bathing figures, sunloud, are shouting
against the blue. their voices float
from ancient danish dublin. it is Thorsday.

Sydney Bernard Smith
from *Girl with a Violin*, Poetry Ireland Editions 3, 1968

FATHER AND SON

Only last week, walking the hushed fields
of our most lovely Meath, now thinned by November,
I came to where the road from Laracor leads
to the Boyne river – that seemed more lake than river,
stretched in uneasy lights and stripped of reeds.

And walking longside an old weir
of my people's, where nothing stirs – only the shadowed
leaden flight of a heron up the lean air –
I went unmanly with grief, knowing how my father,
happy though captive in years, walked last with me there.

Yes, happy in Meath with me for a day
he walked, taking stock of herds hid in their own breathing;
and naming colts, gusty as wind, once steered by his hand,
lightnings winked in the eyes that were half shy in greeting
old friends – the wild blades, when he gallivanted the land.

For that proud, wayward man now my heart breaks –
breaks for that man whose mind was a secret eyrie,
whose kind hand was sole signet of his race,
who curbed me, scorned my green ways, yet increasingly
    loved me,
till Death drew its grey blind down his face.

And yet I am pleased that even my reckless ways
are living shades of his rich calms and passions –
witnesses for him and for those faint namesakes
with whom now he is one, under yew branches,
yes, one in a graven silence no bird breaks.

F.R. Higgins
from *The Gap of Brightness*, Macmillan, 1940

ON THE ELECTION FOR MEATH OF HENRY GRATTAN

The free men of Meath shall never be forgotten,
their names are recorded in the rolls of fame
for how they elected brave Henry Grattan
though dog-hearted tyrants did him defame,
to have him a member of the people assembled
and with him the prime of the country did join.
A shame to the creatures who basely dissembled
when Grattan beat Blythe on the banks of the Boyne.

You paltry usurpers and tyrants take warning,
likewise you mean farmers that cringe to the great,
a stain to your country that auspicious morning
when Liberty called you, you slyly did wait.
The dregs of the people still fail when required,
who barter their honour for interest or coin.
The spirit of freedom within them expired
and faintly withdrew from the banks of the Boyne.

Some are delirious to hear the disaster
and grieve and regret when the tithe's done away;
Oh what will become of the Deacon or pastor?
They'll take an example by Lord Castlereagh.
Too long they have lived on the fat of our nation,
too long these vile creatures our rights did purloin.
Down with oppression and curse extirpation
and shake off your chains on the banks of the Boyne.

Some brighter assailants did terror reform
and rave out their nonsense in the lying meal,
but after a calm there comes always a storm,
such fictions and falsehoods shall never prevail.

'Tis known these past ages how we've been treated,
and Grattan declared with the heart of a lion,
the wrongs of his country he loudly repeated
and bigots gave way on the banks of the Boyne.

James Tevlin (1798–1873)
published in *The Meath Chronicle*, November 5th, 1932

A DROVER

To Meath of the pastures
    from wet hills by the sea,
through Leitrim and Longford
    go my cattle and me.

I hear in the darkness
    their slipping and breathing.
I name them the byways
    they're to pass without heeding.

Then the wet, winding roads,
    brown bogs with black water,
and my thoughts on white ships
    and the King o' Spain's daughter.

O farmer, strong farmer!
    You can spend at the fair;
but your face you must turn
    to your crops and your care.

And soldiers, red soldiers!
    You've seen many lands
but you walk two by two
    and by captain's commands.

O, the smell of the beasts,
    the wet wind in the morn,
and the proud and hard earth
    never broken for corn.

And the crowds at the fair,
    the herds loosened and blind,
loud words and dark faces
    and the wild blood behind.

(O strong men with your best
　　I would strive breast by breast.
I could quiet your herds
　　with my words, with my words!)

I will bring you, my kine,
　　where there's grass to the knee,
but you'll think of scant croppings
　　harsh with salt of the sea.

　　Padraic Colum
　　from *Wild Earth*, The Talbot Press, 1950

from THE ONLY JEALOUSY OF EMER

Cúchulainn
(to his charioteer):

> Look, Laoigh, behind –
> civil, sensible women are listening,
> grey daggers in their right hands,
> gold plate on their breasts.
> A fine figure they cut,
> fierce as warriors in their chariots:
> clearly, my wife has changed!

(to his mistress):

> Show no fear and she will not approach.
> Come, sit beside me
> in the sun-warmed prow
> of my great chariot
> and I will protect you from
> all the female hordes of Ulster.
> Though the daughter of Forghall come
> storming with her company of women
> she will not dare lay a hand on me.

John Montague
from *The Faber Book of Irish Verse*, 1974

DUNSANY CASTLE

The twin dunes stand before it and beneath
their tree-dark summits the Skene river flows
an old, divine earth exaltation glows
about it, though no longer battles breathe.
For time puts all men's swords in his red sheath,
and softlier now the air from Tara blows;
thus in the royalest ground that Ireland knows
stands your sheer house in immemorial Meath.

It stands for actions done and days endured;
old causes God, in guiding time, espoused,
who never brooks the undeserving long.
I found there pleasant chambers filled with song,
(and never were the muses better housed)
repose and dignity and fame assured.

Oliver St. John Gogarty
from *Collected Poems*, The Devin-Adair Company, 1954

In Tara's Halls

A man I praise that once in Tara's Halls
said to the woman on his knees, 'Lie still,
my hundreth year is at an end. I think
that something is about to happen. I think
that the adventure of old age begins.
To many women I have said "lie still",
and given everything a woman needs,
a roof, good clothes, passion, love perhaps,
but never asked for love; should I ask that
I shall be old indeed'.

              Thereon the man
went to the Sacred House and stood between
the golden plough and harrow and spoke aloud
that all attendants and the casual crowd might hear:
'God I have loved, but should I ask return
of God or woman, the time were come to die.'
He bade, his hundred and first year at end,
diggers and carpenters make grave and coffin;
saw that the grave was deep, the coffin sound,
summoned the generations of his house,
lay in the coffin, stopped his breath and died.

William Butler Yeats
from *Last Poems*, Macmillan, 1940

A PRAYER

O brooding Spirit of Wisdom and of Love,
whose mighty wings even now o'ershadow me,
absorb me in thine own immensity,
and raise me far my finite self above!
Purge vanity away, and the weak care
that name or fame of me may widely spread;
and the deep wish keep burning in their stead,
thy blissful influence afar to bear, –
Or see it borne! Let no desire of ease,
no lack of courage, faith, or love, delay
mine own steps on that high thought-paven way
in which my soul her clear commission sees:
Yet with an equal joy let me behold
thy chariot o'er that way by others rolled.

William Rowan Hamilton
from *Irish Poets of the Nineteenth Century* selected by
Geoffrey Taylor, Routledge & Keegan Paul, 1951

Winter in Meath

to Tomas Tranströmer

again we have been surprised
deprived, as if suddenly,
of the earth's familiarity

it is like the snatching away of love
making you aware at last you loved

sorrows force their way in, and pain
like memories half contained

the small birds, testing boldness, leave
delicate tracks
                    closer
to the back door

while the cherry flaunts blossoms of frost
and stands in desperate isolation

John F. Deane
from *Winter in Meath*, Dedalus Press, 1985

from CHRISTMAS DAY

XIII

I was in Meath when you phoned at 8.30 a.m.:
'Paul, will you meet me in Dublin at 10.45
outside the Carmelite Church in Beaumont –
around the corner from Beaumont Hospital?'

In the early morning fog I drove across country,
the hills of East Meath and North Dublin,
by way of the Bolies and Stamullen,
The Naul and the Bog of the Ring.

Although I tried to guess why you had phoned
– Had you been sentenced to death by a doctor?
– Had you decided to marry or to become a monk?
– Had you decided to resign?

I did not pry, being grateful to you
for waking me, for being the cause
of my driving along empty roads
in the heat haze of a May morning.

Crossroads after empty crossroads.
No signposts. No traffic signs.
Queen Anne's Lace, furze, white
blossom of blackthorn in fog.

I could not see the tops of the hills
of Bellewstown and Fourknocks.
I'd slept badly but now I felt well.
Filling up with the right kind of emptiness.

I hoped I'd be able to find the church in time.
I knew where Beaumont Hospital was –
having been visiting Colm Tóibín at Christmas:
his circles of friends feasting at his well.

Buckets of time! I pulled in to the large
car park of the Church of the Nativity of Our Lord
at 10.40 and as I scanned the other parked cars
I saw you stand up the far side of the car park.

You circled round my car. Leaning up against it,
your hands on the roof over the passenger door,
you said: 'I've decided to put my head under
    the water.
I want to get baptized – rightly this time.'

I stare down at the ground – pebbles, grass
and – one solitary marigold
wearing its heart on its tongue – its wet, orange
    tongue.
I mutter: 'Good man yourself,'

I glance up at you –
odd man out.
I kick a pebble, staring at the one solitary marigold.
Jesus Christ!

You say that friends have chided you
for your habit of saying 'God bless'.
Henceforth you will be able to say with authority
'God bless.'

You are edgy before the ceremony at eleven.
You whisper: 'I want to pee.' I point out a tree
at a discreet distance from the adjacent primary school.
You step off into the trees at the far end of the church.

The priest comes out a door, shakes hands, smiles:
'Let's be about our business.'
We sit in a tiny oratory with five sanctuary lamps.
He puts on a white stole over pullover and slacks.

The priest hands me his copy of the Jerusalem Bible.
In my trembling witness's 'speaking-in-public voice'
I read from the Gospel of St. John, Chapter 3:
The Conversation with Nicodemus.

'Not to judge the world
but so that through him the world might be saved.
No one who believes in him will be judged;
but whosoever does not believe is judged already.'

Words that scandalise.
I discover that conscience is the courage to improvise.
When the priest asks you to repeat 'Holy Catholic Church'
You change it to 'Holy Catholic *Christian* Church'.

Driving back to Drogheda – to the Tropical Medicine Unit
of Our Lady of Lourdes Hospital –
I am to be vaccinated against Yellow Fever
before my tour of Brazil –

I stop at the Ivory Coast pub in Balbriggan
for a bottle of mineral water.
I glimpse your sockets pop open beneath your bowed skull
casting a warm eye on death.

Late last night reading the racing pages
you saw that in the 2.45 at Nottingham today
Christian Flight is 20 to 1.
Your life is a form of risk. What do you do?

If you were to go through with your baptism and back
    Christian Flight
she would not win!
So what you had to do is go through with your baptism
and not back *Christian Flight*!

'CHRISTIAN FLIGHT SURPRISES' is the headline
in the next day's newspaper.
Your dedication to chance as the ethic of fate;
self-denial, humility, intuition.

'*Christian Flight* completed a rags-to-riches story
with a success in the Bradmore Fillies' Handicap at
    Nottingham yesterday.
The six-year-old battled to a neck victory
over Le Bal at odds of 20 to 1.'

    Paul Durcan
    from *Christmas Day*, Harvill Collins, 1996

HEADFORT PLACE IN MAY

A blackbird ruffles branches
outside Jack Murphy's shop.

Dew drop splash
sparkling like diamonds.

He sips
the perfection of the morning.

Eamon Cooke
from *Berry Time*, Dedalus Press, 2002

The Poets, at Tailteann drouthy, and drouthy at Tara,
favoured jorums of the heather-juice, the mead.
The poets, after St. Patrick, took them to draughting
the brooks and the spring wells in their own fields.
Norse skalds conveyed the wind that shakes the barley,
brewing the poets ale of their own sheaves.
While Normans shipped the claret in Ormond's barrels
when Galway proffered port to courts and seas.

O'Carolan wetted his whistle after his harping
with a glass that was like water, tintless, clear,
though it leaped the lip and skidded the tongue more sharply,
and lit his ending world with morning's gleam.

The bungs are out for Seán Ó Tuama's barrels,
and Seán sees port like Homer's "wine-dark seas"
go pouring down the poets' open hatches
and roll the poets round like wrecked triremes.

*

So, poets from the foothills and the ledgers,
lively around the white wines and the red,
the screw that plies the bottles for you dredges
the silt of years and grapples the foundered dead.
You, heir to Alighieri's face, sip sherry:
over you, by the hundred traceless heads
of the men that lilted the heart of Ireland merry,
the silkfine songs of "Spanish wine" are said.

Behind you, man swivelling a wrist and ferrying
your whiskey down and whispering "Catullus said –"
O'Carolan's swivelling his harper's wrist, and ferrying,
and hurrying with harper's fingers Catullus' tread.
There's Donnacha Rua Mac Namara looming
by the man who made his fame a trilogy's.

And Raftery, fuddle-pated by the boquets,
sighs "Pockets must have filled since I lacked sprees."

Among the living men a man is proving
no-one translated Rahilly only he;
but through the fast-shut door a soul is moving:
"Long ago," lips Rahilly, "Death translated me."
"And Death translated me and my translator"
comes from the bittern's mourner, Cahal Bwee,
"then he bustled the blackbird boy, was the third lamenter,
up onto the Heavenly Plain, by the way 'twas Meath."

(O yellow bittern, yours was a brilliant ending;
it bound in a ghostly friendship three like these:
your corpse on the ice took the eyes of three good verse-men;
the last is a dust by the side of the Grecian seas.
Whisper! Old Cahal Bwee Mac Gilla Gunna
turns lovely mourning for your drouthy throat;
Ledwidge renames you, keening for Tom MacDonagh
who keyed the mourning to another note).

Now Cahal Bwee's long dead who made strong music;
Thomas MacDonagh dead, who made it new;
Ledwidge, the blackbird, drowned in the loud bugles …
ghosts of these poets come and go with you –
son to the one and heir to the three dead men –
under your lowest murmur murmuring, "We
bid you end quick-limed song, and song whose ending
drowned in the battle-horns by the Greek sea."

Look, through the live men's talk and the dead's miming
another poet's ghost comes lumberingly,
one who's still body-clumsy and clogged with writhing
rhythms unpurged before the soul shot free.
Listen: "No poet here has seen this wonder.

O if he could only bear it, being alive,
my soul would flow above his ear and murmur,
'So... It was shown me since the day I died.'"

Poets that come from foothills and from ledgers,
poets rooted in grasslands and in stones,
singer whose father sang and foretold terrors,
and riming men looted of eyes and bones –
here where the glass tilts and the lip pouches
and the coin chinks through the dribbled, lancing words,
I, with a written verse and a glass, salute you:
Spirits, and living men, with the mouths of birds.

Roibeárd O Faracháin (Robert Farren)
from *Poems of Ireland*, The Irish Times, 1944

A Winter Solstice

A low sun leans across
the fields of County Meath
like thirty watts behind
a dirty blind. New Year begins to breathe
new life into the ground.
The winter wheat begins to teethe.

The tarmac streams like precious ore
beside wrapped bales bright in the glare.
Crows shake like collies by a puddle
blooms of spray, and they declare –
a boy's voice breaking in the throat
of morning – a prayer

that works to scour the slate
of unimaginable
hurt. We draw breath in the air –
its shapes are almost tangible –
and the breath and sweat of horses
makes a minor mist – beautiful.

And beautiful the light on water
as the age's newly minted coin.
You'd be hard pressed from here
to tell a withered elm across the Boyne
from an ash that's hibernating.
Past and present join

in the winter solstice.
The days will stretch and we survive
with losses, yes, and lessons too,
to reap the honey of the hive
of history. The yield of what is given
insists a choice – to live; to thrive.

Peter Fallon
from *The Company of Horses*, The Gallery Press, 2007

Notes

MIDE

Royal Irish Academy Todd Lecture Series Volume IX The Metrical Dindshenchas Part II, Dublin, Hodges, Figgis & Co. Ltd, 1903, reprinted 1941. This poem is attributed in The Book of Leinster to Aed úa Carthaig.

from KING ALFRED'S POEM

"Mileadhach is on the brink of the Barrow at the Meeting of the Three Waters. Sliabh Mairge, now Slewmargy, in the Queen's Co. is the boundary of the Diocese of Ossory at this day. Grian Airbh, the situation of which is as yet unknown to me, must lie on the confines of Tipperary and Kilkenny Counties. The Cross of Grian Airbh divided the Diocese of Ossory or Kilkenny from the Archdiocese of Cashel."

from *Ordnance Survey Letters County Offaly 1838* by John O'Donovan.

THE SHAMROCK HOTEL

The source of this ballad is the Folklore Commission's Schools Project 1937 for Longwood National School. The ballad was composed by Patrick Cullen, told by Patrick Keegan and written down by Barney Keegan, Clondalee, Hill of Down. A note on the original manuscript states that *'The Shamrock Hotel was a lodging house for tramps in Longwood.'*

I REMEMBER SIR ALFRED

The neolithic tumulus at Dowth is east of Slane. Wilde, in 1849, described the tiny structure on the top as a tea house built by Viscount Netterville (*The Beauties of the Boyne and Blackwater*, McGlashan & Gill, 1849, p.204,). Cogan censured Wilde for this facetious comment and explained the structure as a vantage point erected by John, sixth Viscount Netterville (1744–1826), to enable him to follow key stages in the Mass being celebrated in the nearby penal-days chapel. According to Cogan (*History of the Diocese of Meath*, Joseph

Dollard, 1867, ii, p.306) the Catholic viscount followed
the progress of the Eucharist by means of a flag signalling
system operated by his servant down at the chapel.

BELLEWSTOWN RACES

This ballad appeared in the June, 1874 issue of *The Lamp*, and
was republished on the front page of *The Nation* newspaper
on June 13th, 1874.

MAGH BREAGH

These lines appear in *The Story of the Kingdom of Meath* by
Brigid Redmond, Browne & Nolan Ltd., Dublin, n.d.

THE RAM

This song has travelled widely and many versions exist. Most
recently heard on *The Art of Field Recording Volume 1: 50 Years
of Traditional American Music Documented* by Art Rosenbaum,
recorded under the title *Darby's Ram*.

THE SONG OF MARY CRUISE

"In his student days, while walking in the Temple Gardens,
London, [Sir Thomas Plunkett] saw a beautiful girl washing
clothes in the river.... Hearing her sing softly in Irish, with
which he was familiar, he drew a little nearer and recognised
the song as *The Lament of Mary Cruise*... the last person
who knew [the song] in its entirety was an old man named
Paddy Daly, of An Uaimh, who died in the middle of the last
century."

> *A Short History of County Meath*, Donnchad O'Meachair, 1928,
> ps.90–91.

BLUEBELLS FOR LOVE

First published as *Bluebells* in the June, 1945 issue of *The Bell*,
the poem was inspired by Hilda Moriarty, a student of
medicine in UCD from Kerry. The poem was written after a

walk through woods at Dunsany in May 1945 on a visit to the 18th Lord Dunsany, playwright and author, from whom the poet hoped to gain patronage.

A PRAYER

Sir William Rowan Hamilton lived at Dominick Street, Trim, during his early years. His discovery of quaternions in 1843 changed the course of modern algebra.

Index of First Lines

Biographical Notes

ARCHER, PATRICK (1866–1949), writer and Gaelic League activist, assisted with the production of *An Claidheamh Soluis*. His publications include *The Humours of Shanwalla* (1922) and *Fair Fingall* (published posthumously in 1975).

BOLAND, EAVAN, b. 1945, collections include *New Collected Poems* (W.W. Norton & Co. 2008), *Domestic Violence*, (2007), *Against Love Poems* (2001), *The Lost Land* (1998), *An Origin Like Water: Collected Poems 1967–1987* (1996), *In a Time of Violence* (1994), *Outside History: Selected Poems 1980–1990* (1990), *The Journey and Other Poems* (1986), *Night Feed* (1982), and *In Her Own Image* (1980).

BOLGER, DERMOT, b. 1959, collections include *External Affairs* (2008), and he devised and edited the poetry anthology *Night & Day: Twenty Four Hours in the Life of Dublin* in 2008.

CARSON, CIARÁN, b. 1948, collections include *The Irish for No* (The Gallery Press 1987), *Belfast Confetti* (The Gallery Press 1990), and *First Language* (The Gallery Press 1993), *Collected Poems* (The Gallery Press 2008), and *On The Night Watch* (The Gallery Press 2009). Among his prose works are *The Star Factory* (Granta 1997), *Fishing for Amber* (Granta 1999), and *The Pen Friend* (Blackstaff Press 2009).

CLARKE, AUSTIN (1896–1974), one of the leading poets in the generation after Yeats, his *Collected Poems*, edited by R. Dardis Clarke, was published by Carcanet in 2008.

COLUM, PADRAIC (1881–1972), published over fifty books of poetry, fiction, drama, nonfiction, children's literature, and folklore. He also taught at Columbia University from 1939.

COOKE, EAMON, b. 1944, his first collection *Berry Time* was published by Dedalus Press in 2002.

CULLEN, PATRICK, b. 1882/3, a native of the townland of Posseckstown, Enfield. Other songs by him may survive but this is the only one in print.

DEANE, JOHN F., b. 1943, recent collections include *Manhandling the Deity* (Carcanet 2003), *The Instruments of Art* (Carcanet 2005), and *A Little Book of Hours* (Carcanet 2008).

DEANE, SEAMUS, b. 1940, collections include *Gradual Wars* (The Gallery Press 1972), *Rumours* (The Gallery Press 1977), *History Lessons* (1983), and the celebrated novel *Reading in the Dark*.

DURCAN, PAUL, b. 1945, collections include *The Art of Life* (Harvill Secker 2004), *The Laughter of Mothers* (Harvill Secker 2008) and *Life is a Dream* (Harvill Secker 2009).

EGAN, DESMOND, b. 1936, collections include *Midland* (1972), *Leaves* (1974), *Siege!* (1976), *Athlone?* (1980), *Seeing Double* (1983), *Collected Poems* (1983, 1984), *Poems for Peace* (1986), *A Song for my Father* (1989), *Peninsula* (1992), and *Famine* (1997).

FALLON, PADRAIC (1905–1974), publications include *Collected Poems* (Gallery/Carcanet 1990) introduced by Seamus Heaney, edited by Brian Fallon, and *A Look in the Mirror and Other Poems*, introduced by Eavan Boland (Carcanet 2003).

FALLON, PETER, b. 1951, recent publications are *The Company of Horses* (The Gallery Press 2007), *Air and Angels* (Press on Scroll Road 2007) and *Morning Glory* (Warwick Press 2006). *Virgil: Georgics* was published by Oxford University Press in its World's Classics series in 2006.

FANNING, GERARD, b. 1952, his collections with Dedalus Press are *Easter Snow* (1992), *Working for the Government* (1999) and *Water & Power* (2004).

FERGUSON, SAMUEL (1810–1886), was called to the Irish Bar in 1838 and became Deputy Keeper of the Records of Ireland in 1867. *The Poems of Samuel Ferguson* was edited by Padraic Colum and published by Allen Figgis in 1963.

FRENCH, TOM, b. 1966, has published two collections *Touching the Bones* (The Gallery Press 2001) and *The Fire Step* (The Gallery Press 2009).

GOGARTY, OLIVER ST. JOHN (1878–1957), writer, wit, and raconteur, his three volumes of memoirs *As I Was Going Down Sackville Street* (1937), *Tumbling in the Hay* (1939), and *It Isn't This Time of Year at All* (1954), continue to be read.

GREGORY, PADRAIC (1886–1962), publications include *Old World Ballads* (David Nutt 1937), *Ulster Songs and Ballads* (The Talbot Press 1920), and *Complete Collected Ulster Ballads* (W. Mullan 1959).

HAMILTON, WILLIAM ROWAN (1805–1865), one of the most imaginative mathematicians of the nineteenth century, his early years were spent in Trim.

HEANEY, SEAMUS, b. 1939, recent publications are *The Testament of Cresseid & Seven Fables* (Faber 2009), *District and Circle* (Faber 2006), and *Electric Light* (Faber 2001).

HIGGINS, F.R. (1896–1941), collections include *Island Blood* (1925), *The Dark Breed* (1927), *Arable Holdings* (1933), and *The Gap of Brightness* (Macmillan 1940).

KAVANAGH, PATRICK (1904–1967), *Collected poems*, edited by Antoinette Quinn, was published by Penguin in 2004. *A Poet's Country: Selected Prose*, edited by Antoinette Quinn, was published by The Lilliput Press in 2002.

KELLEHER, JOHN V. (1916–2004), Professor of Irish Studies in the Department of Celtic Language and Literatures at Harvard, Richard

Ellmann, in his introduction to his *James Joyce* (1959), describes him "as perhaps the most knowledgeable American on Irish subjects."

KERRIGAN, ANTHONY (1919–1991), translator of Spanish and Latin American writers and senior guest scholar at the University of Notre Dame and the University of Indiana, his collections are *Lear in the Tropic of Paris* (1952), *Espousal in August* (Dolmen Press, 1968) and *At the Front Door of the Atlantic* (Dolmen Press, 1969).

KINSELLA, THOMAS, b. 1928, the author of over thirty collections of poetry, and translations from the Irish, notably the great epic *The Tain*. He was a director of the Dolmen Press and Cuala Press, Dublin, and in 1972 founded Peppercanister Press for the publication of sequences and long occasional poems. Editor of *The New Oxford Book of Irish Verse* and of Austin Clarke's *Selected Poems* and *Collected Poems*, in 2007 Thomas Kinsella was awarded the Freedom of the City of Dublin.

LAVIN, MARY (1912–1996), among her many books are *Tales from Bective Bridge*, with a preface by Lord Dunsany, (Michael Joseph 1943), *The Patriot Son and other stories* (Michael Joseph 1956), *A Memory & Other Stories* (Constable 1972), and *Selected Stories* (Penguin 1984).

LEDWIDGE, FRANCIS (1887–1917), a native of Janeville, Slane, he lived to see one collection *Songs of The Fields* (1916) in print and perished in Ypres at the end of July 1917.

LONGLEY, MICHAEL, b. 1939, collections include *No Continuing City: Poems 1963–1968*, (Macmillan 1969), *An Exploded View: Poems 1968–1972*, (Gollancz 1973), *Poems 1963–1983* (Secker & Warburg 1985), *The Echo Gate: Poems 1975–1979* (Secker & Warburg 1979), *Gorse Fires* (Cape 1991), and *The Weather in Japan* (Cape 2000). He is editor of *Twentieth Century Irish Poems* (2002).

LYNCH, BRIAN, b. 1945, recent publications include *New and Renewed – Poems 1967–2004* (New Island 2004), *Pity for the Wicked* (The Duras Press 2005), and a novel *The Winner of Sorrow* (New Island 2005).

LYNCH, STANISLAUS (1910–1983), publications include *Rhymes of an Irish Huntsman* (Country Life 1937), *Echoes of the Hunting Horn* (The Talbot Press 1946), *A Hunting Man's Rambles* (George Ronald 1951), and *Hounds are Running* (Golden Eagle Books).

Mac CUARTA, SÉAMUS DALL (c.1650–1732/3), a native of the townland of Newstone in the Drumcondra area of north Meath, and one of the most important northern poets of the early eighteenth century.

Mac DONAGH, DONAGH (1912–1968), his poetry publications include *Veterans and Other Poems* (Cuala 1941), *The Hungry Grass* (Faber 1947), and *A Warning to Conquerors* (Dolmen Press).

MacNAMARA, BRINSLEY (1890–1963), playwright and novelist, author of *The Valley of the Squinting Windows* (1918) and *The Clanking of Chains* (1920). His *Growing Up In The Midlands* was published in The Capuchin Annual in 1964.

McAULIFFE, JOHN, b. 1973, his collections are *A Better Life* (The Gallery Press 2002) and *Next Door* (The Gallery Press 2007).

MAHON, DEREK, b. 1941, recent publications include *Adaptations* (The Gallery Press 2006), *Harbour Lights* (The Gallery Press 2005), *Homage to Gaia* (The Gallery Press 2008), *Life on Earth* (The Gallery Press 2008), and *An Autumn Wind* (The Gallery Press 2010).

MEEGAN, PADDY, b. 1922, captained the Meath All-Ireland football team in the 1952 final against Cavan, and was on the victorious 1949 team. His *From the Life Around Me: a selection of poems, stories & memories* was published in 2008.

MONTAGUE, JOHN, b. 1929, his major publications include *The Rough Field* (Dolmen Press 1974), *The Great Cloak* (Dolmen Press 1978), *The Dead Kingdom* (Dolmen Press 1984), *Mount Eagle* (The Gallery Press 1988) and *Smashing the Piano* (The Gallery Press 1999). His collections of stories include *Death of a Chieftain* (MacGibbon & Kee, 1964). *Collected Poems* appeared from The Gallery Press in 1995. In 1998 he became the first Ireland Professor of Poetry.

MORAN, LYNDA, b. 1948, her first collection is *The Truth About Lucy* (Beaver Row Press 1985).

MULDOON, PAUL, b. 1951, recent books include *Plan B* (Enitharmon 2009), *Horse Latitudes* ((Faber 2007), *To Ireland, I* (OUP 2004), *Hay* (Faber 1998), *Moy Sand and Gravel* (Faber 2004) and *The End of the Poem* (Faber 2006) – a series of lectures he delivered as Professor of Poetry at Oxford.

MURRAY, TOMMY, b. 1931, a native of Trim, his collection *Counting Stained Glass Windows* was published by Lapwing in 2009. In March 2007 he accepted the prestigious 'People in Community – IT Project Award' on behalf of The Meath Writers' Circle.

NÍ DHOMHNAILL, NUALA, b. 1952, her collections, with translations into English, are *Pharoah's Daughter* (Bilingual, translations by thirteen writers, The Gallery Press 1990), *The Astrakhan Cloak* (bilingual, translations by Paul Muldoon, The Gallery Press 1992) and *The Water Horse* (bilingual, translations by Medbh McGuckian and Eiléan Ní Chuilleanáin, The Gallery Press 1999).

O'BRIEN, PAUL, REV. (1763–1820), great-grandnephew of Turlough O'Carolan. His popular songs, including *The Fort of Breakey*, were composed before 1801 when he entered Maynooth College for the Archdiocese of Armagh.

Ó DIREÁIN, MÁIRTÍN (1910–1988), his main collections are *Rogha Dánta* (1949), *Ó Mórna agus Dánta Eile* (Cló Morainn 1957), *Ar Ré Dhearóil* (Clóchomhar 1962), *Cloch Choirnéil* (Clóchomhar 1967), *Crainn is Cairde* (Clóchomhar 1970), *Ceacht an Éin* (Clóchomhar 1979), *Dánta 1939–79* (Clóchomhar 1980), *Béasa an Túir* (Clóchomhar 1984), *Tacar Dánta / Selected Poems* (Goldsmith Press 1984), and *Craobhóg: Dán* (Clóchomhar 1986).

Ó FARACHAÍN, ROIBEÁRD (Robert Farren) (1909–1984), collections include *Time's Wall Asunder* (Sheed & Ward 1939), *The First Exile* (Sheed & Ward 1944), an epic poem on St. Columcille, *Rime Gentlemen, Please* (Sheed & Ward 1945), and *Selected Poems* (Sheed & Ward 1951).

O'LOUGHLIN, MICHAEL, b. 1958, collections include *Stalingrad: The Street Dictionary* (Raven Press 1980), *Atlantic Blues* (Raven Arts Press 1982), *The Diary of a Silence* (Raven Arts Press 1985), and *Another Nation, New & Selected Poems* (New Island 1994/UK Arc Publications 1996).

O'REILLY, JOHN BOYLE (1844–1890), sentenced to 20 years' penal servitude in Australia, he escaped to America where he became part owner of *The Boston Pilot* newspaper. His published works include *Songs, Legends and Ballads*, *In Bohemia*, and *Moondyne* (a novel).

O'SULLIVAN, SEUMAS (1879–1958), founded *The Dublin Magazine* in 1923 and edited it until his death in 1958. His *Collected Poems* appeared in 1940.

QUINN, JOHN, b. 1941, broadcaster and radio presenter, publications include *Goodnight, Ballivor, I'll Sleep in Trim* (Veritas 2008), and *Meath: The Royal County* (Cottage Publications 2009).

REILLY, PATRICK (1825–1895), the 'Bard of Balnavoran', born in the townland of Mullaghmore, in the north Meath parish of Drumcondra; his *The Rural Harp, Poems and Lyrics, National, Pathetic and Humorous* was printed and published by J. Hughes, 111 West Street, Drogheda in 1861.

SMITH, SYDNEY BERNARD (1936–2008), publications include *Girl with Violin* (Dolmen Press / Poetry Ireland Editions 3, 1968), *Sensualities* (Raven Arts Press 1981) and *Scurrilities* (Raven Arts Press 1981).

SWIFT, JONATHAN (1667–1745), cleric, political pamphleteer, satirist, and author. In March 1699 Swift was instituted to the Rectory of Agher and the Vicarages of Laracor and Rathbeggan, all in the diocese of Meath, which he held until his death.

TEVLIN, JAMES (1798–1873), a native of Billywood, Moynalty, he wrote mainly in English. Local tradition has it that he ended his days in the lodge at Cherrymount.

Úa CÁRTHAIG, AED, he is not explicitly mentioned in the annals, although the Annals of the Four Masters (a 17th century collection) have a death notice for *'In Drúth Ua Cárthaigh, ollamh Connacht'* ('the poet Ua Cárthaig, chief poet of Connacht') for the year 1097, which would fit with the probable date of this poem. 'Mide' is the only poem attributed to Aed úa Cárthaig.

WOODS, MACDARA, b. 1942, publications include *Notes From the Country of Blood-Red Flowers* (Dedalus Press 1994), *Selected Poems* (Dedalus Press 1996), *The Nightingale Water* (Dedalus Press 2001), *Knowledge in the Blood, New & Selected Poems* (Dedalus Press 2001), and *Artichoke Wine* (Dedalus Press 2006).

YEATS, WILLIAM BUTLER (1865–1939), later works include *The Tower and Other Poems* (1928), *Words for Music, Perhaps* (1932), *The Winding Stair and Other Poems* (1933), *New Poems* (1938), and *Last Poems* (1939).

Acknowledgements

Section XIII from *Christmas Day* by Paul Durcan is reproduced by permission of the author c/o Rogers, Coleridge & White, 20 Powis Mews, London W11 1JN. *Winter in Meath* from *Manhandling the Deity* by John F. Deane, and *March 1st, 1847. By the First Post.* from *New Collected Poems* by Eavan Boland, published by Carcanet Press, reprinted by permission of Carcanet Press Ltd. Publication of *Unwanted Apples* by Paddy Meegan, *Newgrange* by Linda Moran, *An Old Boyne Fish Barn* by Gerard Fanning, *Shanlothe* by Tommy Murray, and *Not Yet Begun* by Brian Lynch, is by kind permission of the authors. *Headford Place in May* by Eamon Cooke and *After the Slane Concert: Bastille Day 1987* by Macdara Woods, appear by kind permission of the Dedalus Press. *Rime, Gentlemen, Please* was first published in *Irish Poems of Today* by *The Irish Times*, and published by kind permission of *The Irish Times*. *A Dream of Solstice* by Seamus Heaney is published by kind permission of the author. *Boyne Valley* by Padraic Fallon appears here by kind permission of Brian Fallon. *Dunsany Castle* was published in *The Poems and Plays of Oliver St John Gogarty* (2001). It is reprinted here by permission of the publishers, Colin Smythe Ltd., on behalf of V.J. O'Mara. *Bluebells for Love* by Patrick Kavanagh is reprinted from *Collected Poems*, edited by Antoinette Quinn (Allen Lane, 2004), by kind permission of the Trustees of the Estate of the late Katherine B. Kavanagh, through the Jonathan Williams Literary Agency. *Tara* and *King John's Castle* by Thomas Kinsella were first published by The Dolmen Press and are reprinted in this anthology by kind permission of the author. *The Echo Gate* and *Oliver Plunkett* from *Collected Poems* by Michael Longley, published by Jonathan Cape, reprinted by permission of The Random House Group Ltd. *An Smiota* by Mairtín Ó Direáin was published first in *Tacar Dánta* by The Goldsmith Press in 1984 and is reprinted by kind permission of The Goldsmith Press, Newbridge, county Kildare. *The Names They Had* was published in John Quinn's memoir *Goodnight Ballivor, I'll Sleep in Trim*, by Veritas in 2008 and is reprinted here by kind permission of Veritas Publications, 7/8 Lower Abbey Street, Dublin 1. Publication of *O'Carolan's Complaint* by Ciarán Carson, *Middle Kingdom* by Seamus Deane, *A Winter Solstice* and *Loughcrew* by Peter Fallon, *The Race Field* by Tom French, *St. Patrick's Day* by Derek Mahon, *A Royal Visit* by John Montague, and *An Obair/'The Task'* by Nuala Ní Dhomhnaill (translated by Paul Muldoon) is by kind permission of the authors and The Gallery Press, Loughcrew, Oldcastle, County Meath, Ireland. *I Remember Sir Alfred* appeared in *Why Brownlee Left* (Faber & Faber) and appears here courtesy of Paul Muldoon and Faber & Faber.